WIMBLEDON
2017

The Official Championships Poster 2017, commemorating three major broadcasting anniversaries with the BBC: 90 years since the first radio broadcast from The Championships, 80 years since the first television broadcast, and 50 years since the first colour television transmission.

WIMBLEDON
2017

By Paul Newman

ROLEX

LEGEND!

8 WIMBLEDON VICTORIES.
19 GRAND SLAM® TITLES.

This watch is a witness to a player who stands alone as the greatest in the history of men's tennis. Worn by a legend who continues his incredible journey, rewriting the records, again and again, with his signature precision and grace. Rolex congratulates the incomparable Roger Federer on his historic 8th Wimbledon victory and 19th Grand Slam® title. It doesn't just tell time. It tells history.

OYSTER PERPETUAL DATEJUST 41

CONTENTS

FOREWORD
by Chairman Philip Brook

I would like to welcome you all to the Official Annual of The Championships 2017, in which we celebrate the many things we will remember about the 131st Championships.

Our new Patron, HRH The Duchess of Cambridge, attended the opening day, watching Andy Murray begin the defence of his gentlemen's singles title while also taking the opportunity to visit some important back of house areas, including the Ball Boys and Girls and our new Event Control Room. She returned for the Gentlemen's Singles Final alongside the Duke of Cambridge to witness a piece of Wimbledon history as Roger Federer became the first player to win eight men's singles titles at The Championships.

Britain's Johanna Konta provided one of the matches of the tournament with her defeat of Donna Vekic in the second round, while her win over Simona Halep to become the first British woman to reach the semi-finals since Jo Durie captured the attention of our nation, with a peak of 7.4 million viewers on the BBC. We were also delighted to see Rafael Nadal return to his best here at Wimbledon, his five-set epic against Gilles Muller thrilling both the No.1 Court crowd as well as all those watching around the world.

We were proud to celebrate 50 years since the 'Wimbledon Pro' event, held here at the All England Club in the August of 1967, which heralded the beginnings of the Open era. In recognition of the significance of this event to tennis history, the eight players who took part – or in the cases where a player was sadly no longer with us, their partner – were invited to this year's Championships as Chairman's guests, along with Virginia Wade on the 40th anniversary of her 1977 win. We were also very proud to celebrate several milestones in our relationship with the BBC – 90 years of radio coverage, 80 years of television, and 50 years of colour television.

Congratulations to all our champions, in particular to Roger Federer on the occasion of a record eighth men's singles triumph here at Wimbledon, and a record 19th Grand Slam singles title overall – a quite remarkable achievement. Congratulations also to Garbiñe Muguruza on her first Wimbledon title, the fourth Spaniard to win a singles title at Wimbledon, joining Conchita Martinez – a member of her victorious compatriot's support staff this year – Manuel Santana and Rafael Nadal. And to those who achieved British success – Jamie Murray, who won the Mixed Doubles Championship alongside Martina Hingis, Alfie Hewett and Gordon Reid, who defended their Gentlemen's Wheelchair Doubles title, and Jordanne Whiley, who alongside Yui Kamiji won the Ladies' Wheelchair Doubles title for the fourth consecutive year.

Finally, to all of those who attended or watched The Championships, thank you for your support, and I hope this annual will prove to be a memorable and enjoyable read.

MATCH 2 MATCH 3 MATCH 4

WELCOME TO
THE CHAMPIONSHIPS
2017

INTRODUCTION
By Paul Newman

One of the joys of sport is the sense of renewal that each passing year brings. As the most famous performers of the day head into the sunset, each new dawn brings the prospect of a fresh generation of heroes and heroines. For all the sorrow that might be felt at the dethroning of great champions, there is a sense of excitement at who might follow in their footsteps.

At the start of 2017 men's tennis was preparing for just such a changing of the guard. Roger Federer and Rafael Nadal, the two finest players of their generation, had brought an early end to their 2016 seasons because of injuries. Federer, aged 35, had not won a Grand Slam tournament since 2012, while 30-year-old Nadal had not won one since 2014. Both men seemed to be in long-term decline.

How wrong those perceptions were proved to be. Federer returned at the start of 2017 after a six-month break and promptly won his 18th Grand Slam title at the Australian Open, despite being taken to five sets in three of his last four matches. His opponent in the final? Nadal.

In the spring Federer won the 'Sunshine Double' in Indian Wells and Miami, beating Nadal in the final in Florida. Come the European clay court season Federer took another break in order to focus on his grass and hard court campaigns, whereupon Nadal took the titles in Monte Carlo, Barcelona and Madrid before winning the French Open for the 10th time.

With Andy Murray and Novak Djokovic – the heirs apparent – struggling with fitness issues and winning just three comparatively minor titles between them in the first six months of the year, was the scene set for Federer and Nadal to continue their extraordinary resurgence at The Championships?

The year had started in similar fashion in the women's game as 35-year-old Serena Williams won her 23rd Grand Slam title at the Australian Open, where her 36-year-old sister, Venus, finished runner-up after reaching her first Grand Slam final since 2009. It was only in the subsequent absence of Serena, who did not play again after revealing that she had been in the early stages of pregnancy in Melbourne, that youth had its day at the French Open, where Jelena Ostapenko triumphed just two days after her 20th birthday.

All eyes on Roehampton

Wimbledon feels more like a three-week event these days, such is the increasing global focus on The Championships Qualifying Competition that has been staged at the Bank of England Sports Centre – situated four miles away in Roehampton – since 1947.

For the first time in its 70 years the event was ticketed with 1,000 per day – priced at £5 each – being snapped up online on a first come, first served basis. Another innovation saw television coverage of matches on the main Show Court at Roehampton broadcast to spectators inside the Grounds via a giant video screen, and to fans around the world on wimbledon.com and through the All England Club's broadcast partners.

Anticipation had only been heightened once 2004 Ladies' Singles champion Maria Sharapova, making a return to the sport following a doping ban, announced her intention to try to qualify for the Main Draw, but a thigh injury eventually ruled her out of the competition. The former champion's absence didn't detract from the entertainment on display, however, which saw players of the quality of Croatia's Petra Martic – who'd reached the last 16 at the French Open earlier in the year – on view, not to mention the odd irresistible British storyline.

The previous year Marcus Willis had negotiated qualifying to become an unlikely Main Draw star, but though he was knocked out in the final round this time home fans found another Cinderella figure in Northampton's Alex Ward, who after injury woes became – as world No.855 – the lowest-ranked singles player to qualify for any Grand Slam for 19 years.

Petra Martic (**right**) and Alex Ward (**below**) qualified for the main event but 2016 star Marcus Willis (**far right**) fell at the final hurdle

Serena would not be the only major female player missing at The Championships 2017. Maria Sharapova, having begun her comeback in April after serving a 15-month ban for a doping offence, suffered a thigh injury which ruled her out of Wimbledon's qualifying tournament, her fall in the world rankings having meant that she had not earned direct entry into the Main Draw. With Angelique Kerber, the 2016 runner-up, struggling to live up to her status as the world No.1, the consensus was that the Ladies' Singles Championships would be a more open contest than it had been for years.

Alongside the younger players who would have their chance to shine in the first two weeks of July were some more familiar figures making welcome returns. Nadal, who had been injured the previous summer, and Victoria Azarenka, who had been recuperating from a knee injury in addition to expecting her first child, were both back at the All England Club, as was Petra Kvitova, the 2011 and 2014 Ladies' Singles champion, who had made a remarkable recovery following a horrific knife attack the previous December.

For the second year in succession The Championships would take place against a backdrop of national uncertainty in Britain. Twelve months earlier competition had got under way just four days after the country had voted in a referendum to leave the European Union. This time The Championships started less than a month after a snap General Election had resulted in a hung parliament. The national mood of unease had been heightened by terrorist attacks in London and Manchester and by a shocking fire at a London tower block that had claimed the lives of at least 80 people.

The Championships might at least provide a welcome diversion from such matters. "I feel that people come to watch and want to be entertained and have a day out and enjoy themselves," Murray said going into The Championships. "It's great that people are still going out to do those sort of things."

Wimbledon awoke to the most beautiful dawn on Monday 3 July 2017, the latest start to The Championships since 1896 and the ideal way to greet the opening of the 131st edition of the world's greatest tennis tournament

Practice makes perfect

Aorangi Park, as ever, was a hive of activity prior to The Championships as the top players prepared on its practice courts, with most attention – naturally – focused on defending champion Andy Murray amid speculation about the extent of his troublesome hip injury. While Garbiñe Muguruza talked tactics with her coaching adviser Conchita Martinez, Rafael Nadal worked on his racket and Murray and co. concentrated on their stretching exercises, no-one could have appeared more relaxed than seven-time champion Roger Federer, who was even happy to have his practice session filmed live on various social media platforms before taking questions from his fans.

WIMBLEDON 2017
Gentlemen's Singles Seeds

Andy MURRAY
Great Britain • Age: 30
Wimbledon titles: 2
Grand Slam titles: 3

1

Novak DJOKOVIC
Serbia • Age: 30
Wimbledon titles: 3
Grand Slam titles: 12

2

Roger FEDERER
Switzerland • Age: 35
Wimbledon titles: 7
Grand Slam titles: 18

3

Rafael NADAL
Spain • Age: 31
Wimbledon titles: 2
Grand Slam titles: 15

4

Stan WAWRINKA
Switzerland • Age: 32
Wimbledon titles: 0
Grand Slam titles: 3

5

Milos RAONIC
Canada • Age: 26
Wimbledon titles: 0
Grand Slam titles: 0

6

Marin CILIC
Croatia • Age: 28
Wimbledon titles: 0
Grand Slam titles: 1

7

Dominic THIEM
Austria • Age: 23
Wimbledon titles: 0
Grand Slam titles: 0

8

Kei NISHIKORI Japan	**9**	**Grigor DIMITROV** Bulgaria	**13**
Alexander ZVEREV Germany	**10**	**Lucas POUILLE** France	**14**
Tomas BERDYCH Czech Republic	**11**	**Gael MONFILS** France	**15**
Jo-Wilfried TSONGA France	**12**	**Gilles MULLER** Luxembourg	**16**

Ladies' Singles Seeds

Angelique KERBER
Germany • Age: 29
Wimbledon titles: 0
Grand Slam titles: 2
1

Simona HALEP
Romania • Age: 25
Wimbledon titles: 0
Grand Slam titles: 0
2

Karolina PLISKOVA
Czech Republic • Age: 25
Wimbledon titles: 0
Grand Slam titles: 0
3

Elina SVITOLINA
Ukraine • Age: 22
Wimbledon titles: 0
Grand Slam titles: 0
4

Caroline WOZNIACKI
Denmark • Age: 26
Wimbledon titles: 0
Grand Slam titles: 0
5

Johanna KONTA
Great Britain • Age: 26
Wimbledon titles: 0
Grand Slam titles: 0
6

Svetlana KUZNETSOVA
Russia • Age: 32
Wimbledon titles: 0
Grand Slam titles: 2
7

Dominika CIBULKOVA
Slovakia • Age: 28
Wimbledon titles: 0
Grand Slam titles: 0
8

Agnieszka RADWANSKA Poland	**9**	**Jelena OSTAPENKO** Latvia	**13**
Venus WILLIAMS USA	**10**	**Garbiñe MUGURUZA** Spain	**14**
Petra KVITOVA Czech Republic	**11**	**Elena VESNINA** Russia	**15**
Kristina MLADENOVIC France	**12**	**Anastasia PAVLYUCHENKOVA** Russia	**16**

DAY
1

MONDAY
3 JULY

A

fter his extraordinary performances in 2016 it was probably inevitable that Andy Murray would suffer an adverse reaction in the early part of the following year. However, few would have guessed at the extent of the Wimbledon champion's subsequent travails after he had secured the world No.1 position for the first time following a remarkable end to 2016. Murray had won his last 24 matches in a row and reached the final of 12 of his last 13 tournaments, nine of which he won.

Previous pages: Andy Murray soothed fears about his injury problems by serving up a comfortable opening to the defence of his title on Centre Court

Above: On what proved to be a lovely opening day of The Championships, huge crowds flocked to take every available vantage point around the outside courts

While Murray's patchy form in the first six months of 2017 had been a worry, it was his fitness that was of greater concern as he walked out to maintain the tradition of the defending Gentlemen's Singles champion opening proceedings on Centre Court on the first day.

A tireless worker in training, Murray has a reputation as one of the fittest and strongest players on the men's tour, but his 2017 campaign had been repeatedly interrupted by setbacks. Having been diagnosed with shingles after an early defeat at the Australian Open, he had suffered further bouts of sickness and missed the Miami Open because of an elbow injury.

After rediscovering some form at the French Open, where he reached the semi-finals, Murray then suffered a hip injury after switching to grass. He lost to Jordan Thompson, the world No.90, in the first round of the Aegon Championships at The Queen's Club and was then forced to withdraw from two scheduled exhibition matches. In the week before The Championships he called a total halt to his on-court preparations in the hope that a little rest would help his sore hip to heal.

By the time the draw was made on the Friday Murray was back practising at Aorangi Park, but all did not appear well with the world No.1. While he was able to run to hit shots, he had a pronounced limp when he walked. He practised each day thereafter, but how would he cope on the match court?

The answer was inconclusive. Murray again appeared to walk awkwardly between points, but in the rallies he moved freely enough en route to an emphatic 6-1, 6-4, 6-2 victory over Kazakhstan's Alexander Bublik.

"I feel pretty good," Murray said afterwards, insisting that his limp was not accompanied by pain. "The last few days I had been feeling better each day. Obviously getting out on the match court is a little bit different. The intensity is a little bit higher, but also the adrenaline can numb some pains that you might have. I moved well today."

Centre Court could hardly have wished for a more entertaining opener. Bublik, a 20-year-old qualifier who was playing only his seventh tour-level match, likes to go for spectacular winners. The world No.135's confidence was evident on the opening point as he rushed into the net before putting away an assured volley.

The 6ft 4in Kazakh also loves hitting drop shots but chose that option too often. Murray, who had been given a rapturous welcome by the Centre Court crowd, played with his own customary flair but was simply much more consistent, making just 10 unforced errors to Bublik's 35. Play in the third set was held up twice by the weather, but at no stage did Bublik look likely to rain on the defending champion's parade.

Murray was by no means the only player who went into The Championships nursing an injury. Nick Kyrgios had also been suffering with a hip problem and from the start it was clear that the No.20 seed was struggling against France's Pierre-Hugues Herbert. After 65 minutes, with Herbert leading 6-3, 6-4, the

Wimbledon lost one of its star attractions early on as Australian Nick Kyrgios, struggling with a hip problem, was forced to retire when two sets down to France's Pierre-Hugues Herbert

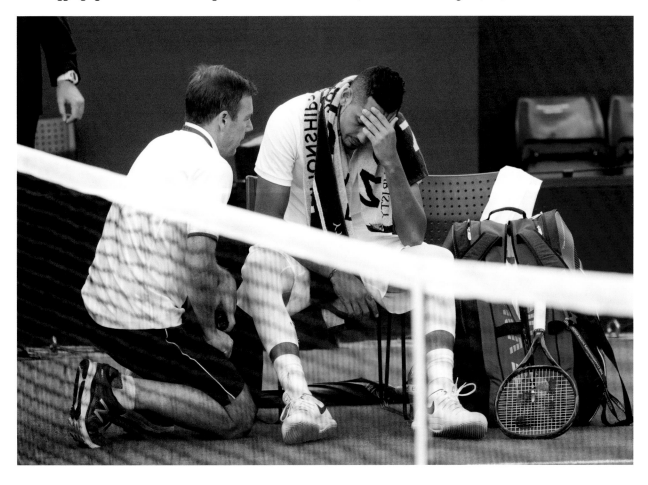

The first real shock of the tournament saw triple Grand Slam winner Stan Wawrinka (**above right**), the world No.3, beaten by rising Russian star Daniil Medvedev (**above left**) on the youngster's Centre Court debut

Australian retired. "It's my favourite tournament," a rueful Kyrgios said afterwards. "It's tough for me to go out there and get beaten and pull out."

Stan Wawrinka was another member of the walking wounded. The No.5 seed had arrived knowing that victory at The Championships would see him become only the ninth man in history to win all four Grand Slam singles tournaments. However, Wawrinka, like Murray and Kyrgios, had lost in the first round at Queen's and was dealing with a long-term problem with his left knee, which he said was aggravated by playing on grass.

It was not the state in which to face Daniil Medvedev, a 21-year-old Russian regarded as one of the best of his generation. The world No.49, who had already won nine matches in a productive grass court campaign but was playing in only his third Grand Slam tournament, won 6-4, 3-6, 6-4, 6-1, after which he knelt down to kiss the playing surface.

Rafael Nadal also knows that grass can be a problem for his knees and did not sound particularly optimistic despite a resounding 6-1, 6-3, 6-2 win over Australia's John Millman in his first match at The Championships for two years. "My knees are ready for the second round probably, that's all," the Spaniard said afterwards.

One of the game's big servers, Marin Cilic, eased to a 6-4, 6-2, 6-3 victory over Philipp Kohlschreiber, but another, Ivo Karlovic, the world No.23, fell at the first hurdle to Britain's Aljaz Bedene, the world No.58. Their world rankings provided just one of the discrepancies between the two men. At 27 Bedene was 11 years younger than Karlovic, who at 6ft 11in stood 11in taller than the Briton.

Karlovic hit 44 aces, adding to his world record total of more than 12,000, but Bedene also served well and won 6-7(5), 7-6(6), 7-6(7), 6-7(7), 8-6. It was the first singles match at The Championships for 15 years to feature four tie-breaks. Bedene finally secured victory by breaking Karlovic after the first 61 games had gone with serve.

Wimbledon's new patron

Perhaps the most welcome of first day visitors to The Championships was HRH The Duchess of Cambridge, who in her new position as Patron of the All England Club enjoyed the chance to meet a host of past and present stars – including Martina Navratilova, Kim Clijsters, Dominic Thiem and Feliciano Lopez – before taking in Andy Murray's opening match on Centre Court.

The Duchess, accompanied by Philip Brook, Chairman of the All England Club, also had time to meet and thank some of the unsung heroes of Wimbledon, including representatives of the British Army, Royal Navy and London Fire Brigade, who act as Service Stewards for The Championships, alongside representatives from the security and ambulance services.

And on being introduced to a few of Wimbledon's Ball Boys and Girls, the Duchess enthused: "Your work makes the game happen. It makes such a difference to the players, your professionalism."

Bedene, born in Slovenia but based in Britain since 2008, became a British citizen in 2015, though his attempts to become eligible for Davis Cup duty for his adopted country had failed because he had already represented the nation of his birth. "I love Britain," Bedene said after his victory, admitting that the noisy support on No.3 Court had given him goosebumps. "I'm a British citizen and I love playing here. It was fantastic being out there."

The opening day was a good one for British tennis. Although Laura Robson, Naomi Broady and Cameron Norrie were beaten by Beatriz Haddad Maia, Irina-Camelia Begu and Jo-Wilfried Tsonga respectively, Johanna Konta and Heather Watson joined Murray and Bedene in the second round.

Like Murray, Konta had gone into The Championships with doubts over her physical condition. The world No.7 had hurt her spine in a heavy fall during her victory over Angelique Kerber at the previous week's Aegon International at Eastbourne that had forced her to withdraw before her scheduled semi-final. It was only on the day before The Championships that Konta confirmed she would be fit to play, but the 26-year-old Briton looked in good shape in her opening match, beating Chinese Taipei's Hsieh Su-Wei 6-2, 6-2. "I'm feeling well," Konta said after avenging her recent defeat to Hsieh at the same stage of the French Open.

Watson's 6-1, 7-6(5) victory over Belgium's Maryna Zanevska continued the world No.102's upward trend after a difficult year. A run to the semi-finals in Eastbourne confirmed her return to form, while a return to the All England Club put a spring in her step. "I just love it here," Watson said. "If there's one

WELCOME BACK PETRA

Nothing warmed the heart on the opening day of The Championships 2017 more than seeing the return of two-time Ladies' Singles champion Petra Kvitova, back on Centre Court just six months after her career had hung in the balance following a knife attack at her home in the Czech Republic.

HRH The Duchess of Cambridge was among the Centre Court spectators who rose to acclaim the return of the two-time champion

The courage and resilience that the 27-year-old displayed in overcoming terrible injuries to her racket-holding hand prompted outpourings of delight and admiration from her colleagues throughout the game.

Kvitova just shrugged before her Wimbledon return that her ordeal had helped put life into perspective. "If I win or lose the last point, I will still be happy to play," she had said on the eve of her first round match with Johanna Larsson, but once back out on her favourite lawn it was as if she had never been away as she swept to victory 6-3, 6-4.

Applauding her from the players' box was Kvitova's surgeon, Dr Radek Kebrle, who'd been flown over to London by Petra as a thank you for all of his remarkable work in repairing the tendon and ligament damage in her left hand.

Dr Kebrle reckoned the comeback of his "perfect patient" had been astonishing. "I told her that there was high risk that she will not pass and come back, but I would do everything I can to help her recover," he told the BBC. "It was ambitious to see her return here in this space of time, but miracles happen."

And how thrilled Kvitova's peers were to see her back. American Madison Keys summed up how moving her friend's return felt when she said: "Every time I watch her play now, I'm an emotional wreck – crying and everything. It's an amazing, amazing comeback. I don't think there's a nicer person that all of us are cheering for… she's such a champion!"

tournament that I could pick to win, it would be this one. It's just the atmosphere, being at home, on the grass, which is one of my favourite surfaces. It's the most famous tournament in the world. It's amazing to be a part of."

Petra Kvitova was also delighted to be back at Wimbledon. In December she had been attacked in her home in the Czech Republic and suffered horrific injuries to her left hand after fighting off her attacker, who had held a knife to her throat. Doctors initially feared that her career might be over, but the former Ladies' Singles champion never lost belief that she could compete again and returned at the French Open. Having then won the title at Edgbaston's Aegon Classic, the world No.12 made a confident start at The Championships with a 6-3, 6-4 victory over Sweden's Johanna Larsson. "It was beautiful to be back on the beautiful Centre Court, playing my game," she said afterwards. "It was very special for me to feel the energy from the crowd again."

Twenty years after her first appearance at The Championships, Venus Williams beat Elise Mertens 7-6(7), 6-4 to reach the second round for the 18th time. However, two other players of similar vintage failed to progress. Mirjana Lucic-Baroni, the only other player in the ladies' singles apart from Williams who had played at The Championships in 1998, lost to Carina Witthoeft after letting slip a 5-0 lead in the deciding set, while 39-year-old Tommy Haas, making his final appearance 20 years after his debut, was beaten by Ruben Bemelmans.

It's good to talk

Andy Murray found a talkative new friend in Alexander Bublik as they nattered away happily on Centre Court

● **Andy Murray has been used to playing** all sorts of intriguing characters in his career but none of them had ever wanted to have a chat with him during the match quite like his lively first round opponent, Kazakhstan's Alexander Bublik, a fact that quite tickled the defending champion.

Earlier in the season the young Kazakh character had done a tongue-in-cheek interview with Murray for a website video feature and asked for any advice 'Sir Andy' could offer. A playful Murray replied that it would help if Bublik didn't serve 20 double faults in a match!

So, before they went out for the third set with Murray comfortably leading, the Scot was taken aback when Bublik, who had been struggling with his serve, turned to him and said: "Yeah, thanks for the advice about not serving 20 double faults!"

Murray smiled: "You served a few", to which Bublik responded: "Yeah, I think I'm only on about 10 right now."

Which, of course, left Murray with the last word: "Well, there's still time to get to 20!" For the record, Bublik finished with 12.

● **A 6-1, 6-3, 6-2 scoreline** may not look great on paper but the bare statistics do not do justice to John Millman's efforts to stick with a rampant Rafael Nadal on No.1 Court. At one point the Australian Millman stretched the two-time champion in a rally lasting 34 strokes before a winner finally rocketed past him. It turned out to be the longest single exchange in the entire Championships.

● **On the day that Wimbledon's absent** Ladies' Singles champion Serena Williams posted a picture of herself on social media enjoying some hitting practice just a couple of months before being due to give birth, Mandy Minella, a 31-year-old from Luxembourg, actually played in her last professional tournament while halfway through her own pregnancy.

Williams had, famously, won the Australian Open earlier in the year while eight weeks pregnant but Minella revealed

Being halfway through her pregnancy didn't prevent Mandy Minella from competing at Wimbledon one last time

the news publicly that she was four-and-a-half months pregnant after losing her first round match at The Championships 6-1, 6-1 to Italy's Francesca Schiavone. The news prompted considerable interest with Minella later posting a lovely photograph of her husband and coach Tim Sommer kissing her baby bump on court.

The world No.82 explained how doctors had been comfortable that it would be safe for both her and her baby if she played. "I enjoy playing and I didn't want to stop," she said. "They said it was fine to play so I wanted to choose the right time to stop. I am happy to finish at Wimbledon, the most prestigious tournament."

Looking after No.1

Five-time champion Venus Williams and Elise Mertens opened proceedings on No.1 Court, with the exciting new look to Wimbledon's second most celebrated arena already starting to take tantalising shape.

Spectators and players alike caught a glimpse of the future with phase one of the complex three-year refurbishment project now having been completed and the new retractable roof beginning to emerge.

For this year's edition of The Championships, the No.1 Court featured a partial fixed roof while retaining a spectator capacity of 11,500, unchanged from last year.

The roof is on course to be completed by The Championships 2019 as part of a project even more complex in both size and scale than the one that transformed and first brought cover to Centre Court in 2009.

As well as the roof, the new-look No.1 Court will feature wider and more comfortable spectator seating, not to mention the addition of two more rows of approximately 900 seats, the creation of a new public

plaza in place of Court 19 – which will open in 2018 – and enhanced and expanded on-site concessions, catering and hospitality facilities.

It has already been a monumental operation with organisers saying the project was akin to "constructing four bridges, then adding 11 bridges on top which move along their own railway". All the fantastic efforts, though, towards creating a second roofed arena will ultimately pay dividends by enhancing Wimbledon's stature as the greatest tennis venue in the world.

DAY
2
TUESDAY
4 JULY

S erena Williams might have been on the other side of the Atlantic preparing for the birth of her first child but the seven-time Ladies' Singles champion was still a regular topic of conversation around the All England Club. The American had been keeping in regular touch with her millions of fans on social media and had even posted a video clip of herself on the opening day of The Championships practising on a clay court while heavily pregnant.

Previous pages: It's all action on the outside courts as the superstars of Wimbledon come out swinging on the second day of The Championships

In Williams' absence it fell to Angelique Kerber, runner-up 12 months earlier, to open the Centre Court programme on the second day. Considering that the world No.1 was facing a qualifier ranked No.247 in the world she might have been expected to go through with a minimum of fuss, but Kerber's error-strewn 6-4, 6-4 victory over the American Irina Falconi rather typified her year.

Kerber had not won any titles since topping the world rankings after winning her second Grand Slam tournament of 2016 at the US Open. She had lost to CoCo Vandeweghe in the fourth round of the 2017 Australian Open, where she was defending the title, and had taken only four games in falling at the first hurdle of the French Open to Ekaterina Makarova.

The 29-year-old German dropped her serve in both sets against Falconi, who has never won a match at The Championships, before closing out victory after an hour and 27 minutes. Kerber said afterwards that remaining at No.1 was proving a tougher task than reaching the top. "There is much more expectation, much more pressure, from me, from outside, from everything," she said.

Kerber and Falconi were the opening act on what had promised to be a fine afternoon's entertainment on Centre Court, with Novak Djokovic and Roger Federer to follow against Martin Klizan and Alexandr Dolgopolov respectively. What transpired, however, was a disappointment to the tournament and spectators alike as Klizan and Dolgopolov both retired early because of injuries they had taken into The Championships.

Djokovic was leading 6-3, 2-0 when Klizan stopped because of a leg injury, while Federer was 6-3, 3-0 up when Dolgopolov retired because of an ankle problem. In drawing up the day's schedule, tournament officials had not been made aware of the two players' fitness issues. "I feel for the crowd," Federer said afterwards. "They're there to watch good tennis, proper tennis."

With the anticipated Centre Court programme over before 5pm, Caroline Wozniacki's match against Timea Babos was promptly added to the schedule. Meanwhile Djokovic joked with Federer in the locker room that they could go out to play a practice set to entertain the crowd, though both agreed that the early retirements of players, which is a problem throughout the game, was a serious issue that needed to be addressed, a view that was reinforced by the All England Club and the tournament executive.

In recent years tournaments have made substantial improvements to the prize money for early losers in recognition of the financial struggles of many lower-ranked players, who can find it hard to make ends meet competing in a global sport. First round losers in singles at The Championships 2017 earned £35,000, more than double what they had been paid five years earlier. While some might consider that to be a lot for losing one match, the counter argument is that the players have earned their place in the Main Draw through their world ranking (which is based on results over the previous 12 months) and therefore deserve the financial rewards.

The pay for first round losers can mean the difference between a player surviving another year on the tour and being forced to give up. Dolgopolov said the prize money was "significant" for anyone outside the world's top 10, while Janko Tipsarevic, who also retired hurt from his first round match, pointed out that one week later players might compete in a Challenger event where they might earn just "150 or 200 euros" and therefore make a substantial loss.

The worry, nevertheless, is that the situation leads to some players starting tournaments despite having injuries which they know might lead to their having to retire hurt mid-match. Spectators are not the only ones to lose out in that scenario, because an injured player's place can be taken by a 'lucky loser' from the qualifying tournament if the withdrawal is made before the match is due to be played.

Federer said: "A player should not go on court if he knows he won't finish. The question always is: should they have started the match at all? In my opinion only the player can really answer that. You hope that they would give up their spot for somebody else, even though they deserve to be in there but fitness is not allowing them."

Left: In the absence of Serena Williams, Angelique Kerber, the 2016 finalist, had the honour of deputising in the defending Ladies' Champion's traditional Tuesday opener on Centre Court, where she defeated America's Irina Falconi

Above: Andre Agassi was all smiles as he passed on his wealth of experience to Novak Djokovic, having joined the three-time Gentlemen's Singles champion's coaching team in May 2017

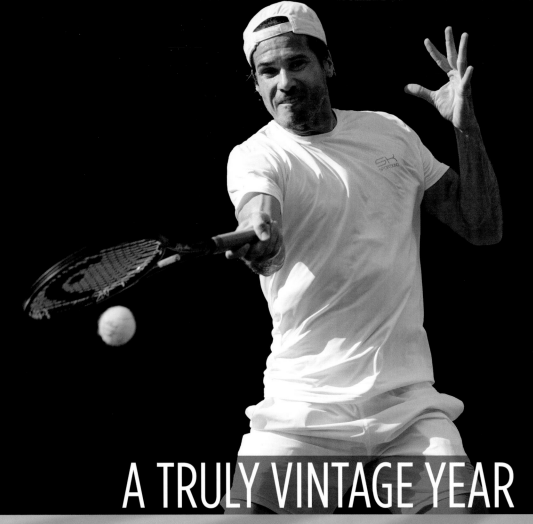

A TRULY VINTAGE YEAR

Tommy Haas, at 39 the oldest player in the Main Draw of either singles event, announced on social media during the second day of The Championships that "the sun set with me @wimbledon last night with my last match" following his defeat by Ruben Bemelmans.

Yet while the popular German was bidding us farewell a whole host of evergreen performers – headed by the champion duo of 35-year-old Roger Federer and 37-year-old Venus Williams (*right*) – were still flying the flag for the 30-something brigade at SW19.

All told, 66 players – 48 men and 18 women – aged 30 and over featured, demonstrating the increased fitness, stamina and durability of seasoned competitors in the 21st century game.

Williams was the oldest player in the ladies' singles draw, just six days older than another first round winner Francesca Schiavone, while Ivo Karlovic (*right*) – the second oldest man at 38 – was still crashing down huge services for fun, although despite hitting 44 aces he found himself on the wrong end of a first round five-set defeat by Britain's Aljaz Bedene.

Spain's 35-year-old Feliciano Lopez protected his proud record by starting a 62nd consecutive Grand Slam – the longest active streak of any current player – but was forced to withdraw in the fourth set of his opening match with Adrian Mannarino through injury.

Yet his 35-year-old compatriot David Ferrer, the indefatigable players' player, was still going strong, producing one of the performances of the first round to beat No.22 seed Richard Gasquet on Court 12.

The Association of Tennis Professionals, which runs the men's tour, has been experimenting with a trial rule whereby players who pull out with an injury after the draw but before their opening match can, at two events in the year, still receive their prize money. There is by no means universal agreement on this – critics say it is wrong to pay someone for not playing – but Federer suggested the scheme might eliminate half of the current first round retirements.

By the end of the second day seven players had thrown in the towel in the gentlemen's singles, which equalled the record number of first round retirements at The Championships in the Open era, set in 2008. Nick Kyrgios, Denis Istomin and Viktor Troicki had all retired early on the first day and were followed by Klizan, Dolgopolov, Feliciano Lopez (who went on to play in the doubles) and Tipsarevic. Only one player, Pablo Cuevas, had withdrawn from the gentlemen's singles before playing his first match, thus denying himself the chance to earn £35,000. There was one first round retirement in the ladies' singles, the 16-year-old Russian Anastasia Potapova suffering a leg injury in a fall when playing Tatjana Maria.

Federer had only 42 minutes on court (two more than Djokovic) but still found the time to pass two milestones. His 85th match win at The Championships took him one past Jimmy Connors, with whom he had previously shared the Wimbledon men's record, while his 10 aces saw him become only the third man, after Goran Ivanisevic and Ivo Karlovic, to pass the 10,000 mark in the 26 years since the ATP started recording the statistics.

Meanwhile Djokovic's player's box looked very different to past years. The Serb dismissed his entire coaching team during the spring before asking Andre Agassi, the 1992 Gentlemen's Singles champion, to join his entourage. He was also assisted by Mario Ancic, who reached the semi-finals at The Championships in 2004.

Qualifiers produced two of the finest performances of the second day as Australia's Arina Rodionova and Croatia's Petra Martic both knocked out seeds. Rodionova saved seven match points before beating the No.16 seed, Russia's Anastasia Pavlyuchenkova, 3-6, 7-6(6), 9-7, while Martic beat the No.20 seed, Australia's Daria Gavrilova, 6-4, 2-6, 10-8. For the most part, however, the leading lights in the ladies' singles made assured progress. Karolina Pliskova, continuing her pursuit of Kerber at the top of the world rankings, beat Evgeniya Rodina 6-1, 6-4, while Garbiñe Muguruza, Svetlana Kuznetsova and Agnieszka Radwanska enjoyed straight-sets victories over Ekaterina Alexandrova, Ons Jabeur and Jelena Jankovic respectively. Wozniacki had to resist a fightback by Babos before easing to a 6-4, 4-6, 6-1 victory.

Kyle Edmund, who defeated qualifier Alex Ward in a rare all-British singles contest, was one of five Britons to advance to the second round

Getting the headband back together

If you wanted to get ahead at this year's Wimbledon, a head really needed a bandana. Or a headband. Or a sun visor. Indeed, you might even have been persuaded that as Pat Cash was back on the courts in a coaching capacity, the profusion of headbands on display could have been a retro tribute to one of The Championships' favourite Australian visitors. Of course, Roger Federer, Rafael Nadal and Kei Nishikori have long been 'band leaders', but it was good to see the likes of US teenager Frances Tiafoe (*opposite, top left*) and Latvia's French Open champion Jelena Ostapenko giving the headband a youthful fillip too, a look that was also seen amongst some of the more exuberant spectators around the Grounds. Elsewhere CoCo Vandeweghe plumped for a sun visor rather than model her own version of her coach Cash's headband, an approach that was mirrored in hair-raising fashion by Britain's Katie Boulter (*right*).

By the end of the day there were no Australians left in the gentlemen's singles competition. Following defeats for Kyrgios, Andrew Whittington and John Millman on the first day, Bernard Tomic went down in lacklustre fashion to Mischa Zverev, Thanasi Kokkinakis had the misfortune to be drawn against Juan Martin del Potro and Jordan Thompson was beaten by Albert Ramos-Vinolas. It was only the second time since the Second World War that Australian men had failed to win a match in singles, the other occasion having been in 2012. While several of the Australians had tough draws it was still an ignominious day for a country with such a rich history of success. Only the United States and Britain have won more gentlemen's singles titles at The Championships.

The Americans, in contrast, celebrated Independence Day by taking their representation in the second round of singles to 10 women and eight men. Sloane Stephens, who lost to her compatriot Alison Riske, was not among them, but was just happy to be playing again after nearly a year on the sidelines with a foot injury.

Kyle Edmund became the fifth British player to clear the first hurdle, beating his fellow countryman, Alex Ward. It was only the second all-British encounter in the gentlemen's singles since 2001. Of the other Britons, James Ward and Brydan Klein lost in straight sets to Marcos Baghdatis and Yuichi Sugita respectively, while 20-year-old Katie Boulter, making her debut in the Main Draw, lost in three sets to the experienced American, Christina McHale.

Milos Raonic, the previous year's runner-up, hit the fastest serve of the tournament so far – an impressive 141mph – in beating Jan-Lennard Struff in straight sets, while David Ferrer, aged 35, turned back the clock to knock out Richard Gasquet, the No.22 seed. Ernests Gulbis, who had dropped out of the world's top 500 after a succession of injuries, won a tour-level match for the first time in more than a year when he beat Victor Estrella Burgos 6-1, 6-1, 6-2. His win appeared all too much for one of the Ball Girls out on Court 16 who fainted in the 23C heat. It was a prelude of what was to come as both the air temperatures and the heat of competition kept rising in the days that followed.

As the afternoon shadows lengthened on Court 12, Grigor Dimitrov was in no mood to hang around as he beat Argentina's Diego Schwartzman in straight sets

10,000 and counting

Roger Federer and Ball Boy Haris Khan show off the ball with which the Swiss legend struck his 10,000th ace

CHAMPIONSHIPS Day 2 NOTEBOOK

• **Roger Federer served the 10,000th ace** of his professional career in his match against Alexandr Dolgopolov, and the Ball Boy who was later discovered to be the one who collected the historic ball received the shock of his life while he was relating the story of his big moment to The Wimbledon Channel.

Young Haris Khan's face was a picture when he discovered the fellow interrupting his tale to thank him turned out to be none other than Federer himself, and the teenager thought it an excellent idea when the great Swiss – who used to be a Ball Boy himself – suggested they put the landmark ball up for auction to raise money for the Wimbledon Foundation.

• **It can be a precarious business** being a line umpire when servers are hammering the ball down at speeds in the region of 140mph and it certainly proved a difficult day for one official in the firing line as Juan Martin del Potro and Thanasi Kokkinakis went to work. The gentleman in question did not just get hit once but three times in all from booming serves straight down the T. Despite it all, showing true stoicism, he just got on with his job.

• **Bernard Tomic, the talented and enigmatic** Australian player, became the centre of attention with a remarkably frank interview following his 6-4, 6-3, 6-4 first round loss to Mischa Zverev, claiming that he had felt "bored" during the match and wasn't really concerned by his results.

The 24-year-old, who was also later to be fined $15,000 (£11,600) by the Grand Slam Supervisors after he admitted calling for the trainer even when he was not injured in a bid to disrupt his opponent's momentum, said: "I couldn't care less if I make a fourth round at the US Open or I lose first round.

"To me, everything is the same. I'm going to play another 10 years, and I know after my career I won't have to work again."

The comments prompted an unsurprising backlash with Tomic's racket sponsors HEAD later announcing the end of their association with him. Some of the greats of the sport also weighed in, with Martina Navratilova saying his comments were "disrespectful to the sport".

Australia's Bernard Tomic made some controversial remarks in his post-match media conference

• **Grigor Dimitrov, who opened with an impressive win** over Argentina's Diego Schwartzman, talked afterwards of how he had prepared the previous weekend by helping coach Romeo Beckham, the 14-year-old son of retired England superstar David Beckham, who has shown an aptitude for tennis after deciding not to follow in his dad's footballing steps.

"Romeo, he's a very talented kid," noted the impressed Bulgarian, who has become firm friends with the Beckham family. "I think he hasn't played tennis for that long, but he sure showed a lot of potential." Watch this space...

DAY
3

WEDNESDAY
5 JULY

O n a sun-kissed day when the temperature reached 30C, Johanna Konta was no doubt grateful for all her experience growing up in the heat of Sydney, where she spent the first 13 years of her life. The 26-year-old Briton was tested to the limit, both physically and mentally, before beating Donna Vekic 7-6(4), 4-6, 10-8 in a contest which she described as "one of the most epic matches I have been a part of".

Previous pages: In beating Wang Qiang, Venus Williams played her 97th match in the Main Draw at Wimbledon, the most of any active female player and one more than a certain Serena Williams

For all her progress over the last two years, Konta had arrived at The Championships with only one win from her five previous appearances in the Main Draw. Victory in the first round over Hsieh Su-Wei, who had beaten her five weeks earlier at the French Open, earned a second round meeting with Vekic, a 21-year-old from Croatia who had beaten Konta in the final of the Briton's first grass court tournament of the year at the Nottingham Open.

Their Centre Court meeting developed into a thriller, with Konta striking 55 winners to Vekic's 42 in a tense battle between two big hitters. As well as the heat, the players had to deal with an invasion of flying ants, on their customary July outing. "I definitely have taken home a few, both in my belly and in my bags," Konta said after revealing that some of the insects had even flown into her mouth.

Vekic, the world No.58, served for the first set at 5-3 before Konta broke back and edged the eventual tie-break 7-4. After Vekic had taken the second set, the decider was close throughout, with the only break of serve coming in the final game. Konta went 0-30 down on her serve in successive games at 6-6, 7-7 and 8-8 but held firm on each occasion. Vekic saved one match point at 8-9 with an ace but a forehand error on the second gave Konta victory after three hours and 10 minutes. "Both of us deserved to win," the world No.7 said afterwards. "It was a great battle to be a part of."

Compared with many of her rivals, Konta's rise has come late in her career. Only two years previously, when ranked No.126 in the world, she had needed a wild card to play at The Championships before making her big breakthrough with a run to the fourth round of the US Open later in the summer. Konta, whose family moved to Britain in 2005 before she obtained British citizenship in 2012, broke into the world's top 30 after reaching the semi-finals of last year's Australian Open and in October became the first British woman for 32 years to be ranked in the singles top 10. She continued her progress in 2017 by enjoying the biggest victory of her career at the Miami Open.

Konta's Spanish coach, Esteban Carril, who was replaced by the Belgian Wim Fissette at the end of 2016, played an important part in her development, as did Juan Coto, a mind coach who helped her to change from a player who struggled to cope with pressure into one renowned for her mental strength. Whatever else goes on around her, Konta has developed the capacity to remain within what she describes as her "bubble", focusing only on the next point. Coto's sudden death at the end of 2016 was a huge shock, but Konta continued to follow his guidelines and began working this year with another mind coach, Elena Sosa.

While Konta had been marching up the rankings, her predecessor as British No.1, Heather Watson, had been heading in the other direction. Wimbledon's 2016 Mixed Doubles champion went into the 2017 grass court season having not won back-to-back tour-level singles matches for more than a year. She had also fallen out of the world's top 100, which meant having to go back to playing in lesser tournaments.

Left: Johanna Konta had the Centre Court crowd on their feet with some truly glorious shots

Below: Vekic, who had beaten Konta in a similar thriller in the Nottingham Open final, threatened to spoil the script with her impressive power and resilience

Feelin' hot, hot, hot

The soaring temperatures made it a wonderful afternoon to lounge on Aorangi Terrace under a parasol while enjoying a glass of Pimm's and watching the action on the Big Screen, but it made life more challenging for the St John Ambulance teams who were called to deal with spectators suffering from heat-related ailments.

With temperatures tipping 30C in the afternoon and more hot weather forecast for the rest of the week, plans were quickly put into place to introduce the measures Wimbledon reserves for its hottest days, including the more frequent rotation of Ball Boys and Girls while ensuring they wore their special caps with neck flaps to protect them from the sun.

The demand for frozen treats was such that the Media Centre ran out of ice creams and even Rufus the Harris Hawk, the airborne protector of The Championships, was grateful to be doused with a touch of water to keep him cool.

"Your feet get put back on the ground," Watson said. "At one tournament there was no water. At these tournaments you're used to just picking up your water bottles from the fridge and a small thing like that makes such a difference. You get treated so well and they make life so easy for us. Not having water at a tournament, not having a towel, having to leave deposits for tennis balls and giving them back, that was all quite difficult."

A return to the green grass of home lifted Watson's spirits. She reached the semi-finals in Eastbourne, beat Maryna Zanevska in the first round at The Championships and enjoyed an emphatic 6-0, 6-4 victory in the second over Latvia's Anastasija Sevastova, ranked 83 places higher at No.19 in the world, to send two British women into the third round for the first time since 1986. Watson did not make one unforced error in the opening set, which she won in just 19 minutes, and recovered from 3-1 down to take the second. "I'm confident, just really enjoying being out there on the court at the moment," Watson said afterwards.

Victories for Andy Murray, who beat Germany's Dustin Brown 6-3, 6-2, 6-2, and Aljaz Bedene, a 6-3, 3-6, 6-3, 6-3 winner over Bosnia's Damir Dzumhur, ensured that Britain would have at least four singles players in the third round for the first time since 1997, when Tim Henman, Mark Petchey, Greg Rusedski, Andrew Richardson and Karen Cross all reached the last 32. Murray, however, wanted more British success. "Aim as high as you can," he said. "Why not try and get five, six players into the quarter-finals of Slams?"

Having beaten Alexander Bublik in the first round, Murray faced another unpredictable opponent in the second but Brown's drop shots, big second serves, explosive returns and charges into the net failed to unsettle the defending champion. Murray read the German's game with increasing ease and said the sore hip which had disrupted his preparations had not been a problem. "I've moved well," he said. "In the first couple of matches it hasn't affected me and I've been getting in good practices." Brown said: "If he has a problem with his hip, I don't want to play against him when his hip is good."

The 6ft 5in Brown lost on a day when some other big men on tour prospered. Poland's Jerzy Janowicz (6ft 8in), the 2013 semi-finalist, knocked out the No.14 seed, Lucas Pouille, Sam Querrey (6ft 6in) dropped a set before beating Nikoloz Basilashvili and Kevin Anderson (6ft 8in) and Marin Cilic (6ft 6in) enjoyed straight-sets wins over Andreas Seppi and Florian Mayer respectively. Elsewhere, Gilles Muller (6ft 4in) needed five sets and more than three-and-a-half hours to overcome Lukas Rosol (6ft 5in).

Flamboyant German grass court specialist Dustin Brown lived up to his reputation, but Andy Murray was rarely troubled

UNWELCOME VISITORS

W imbledon has known its invasions from all creatures great and small down the years, from the pigeons that once dive-bombed Boris Becker during a match to the swarm of bees that sent picnickers scuttling away from Henman Hill a few years back.

Yet nothing had quite prepared us all for the day when thousands of flying ants descended on the lawns for around an hour, distracting and irritating players and causing a decided nuisance to spectators too.

Talk about being bugged, this was ridiculous reckoned some of the players as they reflected on the curious phenomenon known as 'Flying Ant Day', an annual occurrence which does not usually coincide with The Championships, when the insects – in their reproductive stage – choose to leave their colony in droves in search of a new one.

Out on Court 18 the ants were to be found in such profusion during stages of Sam Querrey's win over Georgian Nikoloz Basilashvili that the big-serving American felt like stopping: "Never seen that before. Luckily it was [only for] 30 or 45 minutes. I don't know what it was, but they seemed to kind of go away after a while. If it had got much worse I almost wanted to stop because they were hitting you in the face when you were trying to hit balls."

Querrey mentioned the problem to the umpire but was told that the show must go on: "He kind of laughed,

'The flowers, the bugs, they're happy', something like that. He kind of shrugged it off. Like, these are just bugs, we're going to play through it!"

Jo-Wilfried Tsonga noted that the ants had got "in my nose, in my hair", while Johanna Konta reckoned a little queasily after coming off that she had probably swallowed more than her fair share of the pesky insects during her epic match against Donna Vekic.

Previous pages: A lovely overhead panorama of the outside courts shows the doubles competitions in full swing

Right: Rafael Nadal flew into the third round with a straight-sets win over American Donald Young on Centre Court

Rafael Nadal, who stands a comparatively modest 6ft 1in tall, won in straight sets for the second round in succession, beating Donald Young 6-4, 6-2, 7-5 with an assured performance that showed again what a good grass court player the 'King of Clay' can be. There was an unlikely postscript to Nadal's match when a fan asked him to sign a prosthetic leg as he left the court and an equally bizarre scene after Ruben Bemelmans' 6-4, 6-2, 3-6, 2-6, 6-3 victory over Daniil Medvedev, Stan Wawrinka's conqueror. Having clashed with Mariana Alves, the umpire, during the match, Medvedev threw coins at the foot of her chair at the end of it. He later apologised for doing "a bad thing" in the heat of the moment and said he could not explain his actions. He was later fined $14,500 (about £11,200) for his behaviour during and after the match.

The No.15 seed, Elena Vesnina, a semi-finalist in 2016, was beaten 3-6, 3-6 by Victoria Azarenka as the former world No.1's comeback gathered pace. Madison Keys, the No.17 seed, was beaten 4-6, 7-6(10), 1-6 by Camila Giorgi, while Carla Suarez Navarro, the No.25 seed, went down 2-6, 2-6 to Peng Shuai. Simona Halep, the No.2 seed, eased to a 7-5, 6-3 victory over Beatriz Haddad Maia, but Jelena Ostapenko, the French Open champion, went within three points of losing to Francoise Abanda before winning 4-6, 7-6(4), 6-3. "I wasn't very happy with the way I played but I'm happy that I could fight and win," Ostapenko said afterwards.

Venus Williams' difficult start continued with a scratchy 4-6, 6-4, 6-1 victory over Wang Qiang. The five-time Wimbledon champion had wept at her press conference following her first round win when she was asked to comment on the police investigation into a recent car crash in Florida in which she was involved – following which a 78-year-old passenger in the other vehicle died. Slow to get going against Wang, Williams defended two break points at 3-3 in the second set before recovering to win nine of the last 11 games.

Petra Kvitova, playing only her third tournament after the terrifying attack on her seven months earlier, was beaten 3-6, 6-1, 2-6 by Madison Brengle, the world No.95. The 2011 and 2014 Ladies' Singles champion, who struggled in the heat and had her blood pressure checked after the second set, said the loss was hard to take given the work she had put into her rehabilitation. However, by the end of the week she was putting things in perspective. "This is only the beginning of my new journey and I will come back stronger," she wrote on social media. "See you next year, my dear Wimbledon."

CoCo's Cashing in

It was good to see Pat Cash's famous headband still in evidence as he coached American hopeful CoCo Vandeweghe three decades on from his Wimbledon triumph

CHAMPIONSHIPS Day 3 NOTEBOOK

● **Wednesday marked the 30th anniversary** of one of Wimbledon's landmark moments. Pat Cash always jokes that nobody remembers that he beat three great players en route to the title in 1987 but that everyone recalls his precarious and unprecedented climb into the stands – and into sporting legend – to hug his family and friends after his win over Ivan Lendl.

That ascent has become a time-honoured tradition but Cash was the pioneer who never knew until he stepped on to the commentary box roof whether he was going to crash through it. "I nearly chickened out," he later admitted, but with true Aussie grit decided to go for broke.

Now 52, Cash is not a big one for anniversaries so didn't celebrate the landmark on the night in question as he had more important business to attend to – coaching the US hopeful CoCo Vandeweghe. Vandeweghe has laughed about Cash's "dorky ways" and joked that he was introducing her to 1980s rock bands – forcing her to gently remind him she was born in 1991 – but she was adamant that the Australian's big day should be remembered: "I hope there is some magic that rubs off on to me," she smiled.

● **Nikoloz Basilashvili may have had a humbling time** at the French Open when eventual champion Rafael Nadal dismantled him 6-0, 6-1, 6-0, but even though he was knocked out by Sam Querrey in the second round at The Championships the Georgian ensured he would end up making a positive mark on Wimbledon by sending down the biggest serve of the entire tournament – a 143mph thunderbolt.

Andy Murray thankfully put in a far sharper performance against Dustin Brown than his namesake could muster at Worcester

● **It was good to see Andy Murray looking sprightly** as he dispatched Dustin Brown on Centre Court but, alas, the same could not be said of the racehorse Murray Mount, who soon before its famous namesake took to the court started the 2.20 at Worcester as the favourite in a handicap steeplechase only to stumble, hit a fence and eventually trail home fourth. It apparently prompted one disgruntled racegoer to suggest it might have run better had it been named Henman Hill!

● **Heather Watson evidently felt** she was doing one of her coaches, Morgan Phillips, a big favour when he got so carried away by her good form that he claimed he would have his head shaved if she went on to reach the second week.

"I said, 'No, your girlfriend will kill you!'" Watson explained. "You can shave your legs instead…"

DAY
4

THURSDAY
6 JULY

W

hile Petra Kvitova's status as the favourite to win the ladies' singles had been questioned by many – on the basis that The Championships had come too soon into her comeback – few doubted Karolina Pliskova's credentials as a potential champion.

The No.3 seed had reached her first Grand Slam singles final on the US Open's hard courts the previous summer and had made the semi-finals on clay at the French Open. Grass, moreover, was potentially the best surface for a big-hitter who had struck more aces than anyone on the women's tour in the first six months of the year. Furthermore, just two days before The Championships, Pliskova had claimed her second grass court title by winning the Aegon International at Eastbourne.

Following Kvitova's second round defeat her fellow Czech was an even warmer favourite for the title, but Pliskova had the misfortune to run into an opponent in equally good form on grass. Magdalena Rybarikova, who beat Pliskova 3-6, 7-5, 6-2 in one of the year's biggest surprises, had begun the grass court season ranked No.192 in the world after missing the second half of 2016 following knee and wrist surgery. However, the 28-year-old Slovakian enjoys playing on grass and went into her second round match on the back of 14 victories in her 15 matches on the surface in 2017, having won the titles at the International Tennis Federation tournaments at Surbiton and Ilkley and reached the semi-finals in Nottingham.

At a set and a break up, nevertheless, Pliskova appeared to be coasting, only for her confidence to evaporate on the hottest day of the Wimbledon Fortnight as the temperature climbed above 30C. Rybarikova became more assured at the net, troubled Pliskova with her sliced backhands and, crucially, played the big points better. Pliskova had 11 break points but converted only three of them, while Rybarikova won five of her six. Rybarikova, who had lost in the first round on eight of her nine previous visits to The Championships, told the BBC afterwards: "It's special. It's amazing. It was very difficult to play Karolina Pliskova. I was not so confident. I had two surgeries and hadn't played for seven months. It was a difficult time for me."

Pliskova described Rybarikova as a "very tricky opponent" to face so early in the competition and added that every round seemed to be difficult at the major tournaments these days. "Maybe before, you won the first three or four matches and you almost didn't have to practise but now it's different," she said. Asked about her record at The Championships, where she has never gone beyond the second round, Pliskova said with a rueful smile: "It's probably something in the air here."

Despite her defeat Pliskova still had a good chance of replacing Angelique Kerber at the top of the world rankings, especially as the German continued to struggle. Although Kerber beat Kirsten Flipkens 7-5, 7-5, the world No.1 was frequently outfoxed by her opponent's clever mix of slices, drop shots and charges into the net in a contest which featured eight breaks of serve. "It was not an easy match," Kerber said afterwards. "Kirsten is always tough to play."

Agnieszka Radwanska, the No.9 seed, was also made to work for her victory and saved two match points before beating Christina McHale 5-7, 7-6(7), 6-3. Daria Kasatkina and Lucie Safarova, seeded No.29 and No.32 respectively, both went out. Anett Kontaveit beat Kasatkina 6-3, 6-2, while Shelby Rogers beat Safarova 6-7(4), 6-4, 6-3. However, Garbiñe Muguruza, Caroline Wozniacki, Svetlana Kuznetsova and CoCo Vandeweghe all enjoyed smooth passages into the third round with straight-sets victories over Yanina Wickmayer, Tsvetana Pironkova, Ekaterina Makarova and Tatjana Maria respectively.

Bethanie Mattek-Sands' day ended in agony when she suffered a serious knee injury at the start of the third set against Sorana Cirstea on Court 17. Mattek-Sands, one of the most colourful players in the women's game and famed for her outlandish dress sense, was running towards the net when her right knee, to which she had suffered a serious ligament injury four years earlier, gave way beneath her. The 32-year-old American lay on the floor screaming in pain after dislocating her right kneecap and rupturing her patellar tendon.

Safarova, Mattek-Sands' doubles partner, watched in tears as her friend, who refused to have the knee tended to on court, was treated for the pain before she was carried off on a stretcher and taken to hospital to have the knee put back into place. Mattek-Sands, who would have held all four Grand Slam ladies'

There was widespread shock around the Grounds over the news of the dreadful knee injury suffered by American Bethanie Mattek-Sands during her second round match with Sorana Cirstea

A HOT SUMMER

A Wimbledon scorched in sunshine may have been wonderful news for spectators, but concerted spells of hot, dry weather inevitably have an impact on meticulously tended grass and therefore pose obvious challenges for Head of Courts and Horticulture Neil Stubley and his staff.

Getting towards the end of a first week in which the Grounds were never spared from the beating sun, a few players complained about the state of the courts being unusually hard, uneven or slippy.

The unrelenting heat after an unusually dry couple of months did appear to take a toll on the grass on court – particularly around the baselines – leading to the most experienced stars like Roger Federer, Novak Djokovic and Andy Murray, when asked by the media, observing different conditions to normal.

"I could see a difference in grass, in the turf itself. It was a bit softer, especially around a couple of feet inside and outside the baseline," said Djokovic.

Yet amid speculation that conditions might become dangerous in the second week, Stubley soothed concerns by explaining: "There's not a doubt in our minds that the courts will be as good as they need to be for the end of The Championships.

"Obviously we're dealing with the extreme heat, which we're not used to. We go into The Championships with as healthy grass as we possibly can, so we can

The Wimbledon groundstaff worked tirelessly throughout an especially hot Championships to ensure all courts were in the best possible condition

endure those extremes. If we get extreme heat – or, as last year, extreme wet – we can deal with it."

Djokovic, for one, was happy the courts were, as ever, in the safest hands. "The groundsmen of Wimbledon are the best in the world, by far, for grass courts," said the triple champion. "So they are making sure to keep the courts in good conditions and well kept."

doubles titles with Safarova if they had won at The Championships, was in tears again two days later when she spoke to her fans on Facebook Live, explaining that she would be returning to the United States for surgery. She described it as "one of the most painful injuries that I've had – and I've had a few in my career".

While the court surface appeared to play no part in Mattek-Sands' injury, Kristina Mladenovic complained about the condition of Court 18 after losing 6-2, 4-6, 4-6 to Alison Riske. Mladenovic said she had twisted her ankle in the warm-up and that both players had been unhappy about the surface. The Frenchwoman said there was no grass left on the baseline, where the surface was uneven and slippery and had "a huge hole" in it. Some players were also unhappy about the state of the baselines on Centre Court.

However, tournament officials who inspected Court 18 following the players' complaints gave it the all-clear, as did Neil Stubley, the All England Club's Head of Courts and Horticulture, who said it was "playable as normal". The Club said in a statement that all the courts had been prepared "to exactly the same meticulous standard as in previous years" and that daily hardness and moisture readings on Court 18 had shown nothing unusual. "Grass is a natural surface and it is usual for the baselines to start to be showing signs of wear and tear four days into The Championships," the Club said.

Belgium's Steve Darcis became the eighth player to retire from the gentlemen's singles when he pulled out with a back injury after only three games against David Ferrer, while Roger Federer and Novak Djokovic were both happy to complete their second round matches following the early retirements of their first round opponents.

Federer beat Serbia's Dusan Lajovic 7-6(0), 6-3, 6-2, but only after an edgy start and an erratic first set. "I was feeling nerves for some reason," Federer said afterwards. "It was definitely more acute than I normally feel. All of a sudden I was walking up to the locker room after my warm-up and I was just feeling excited and nervous. Then when I walked to the court it was still ongoing and after the warm-up it was still there. And down 1-0, 0-40, it was still there. It was still there at 7-6 in the first set. Just took a while to shake it off, to be honest."

Roger Federer soaked up the acclaim of Centre Court once again after dismantling Serbia's Dusan Lajovic in straight sets

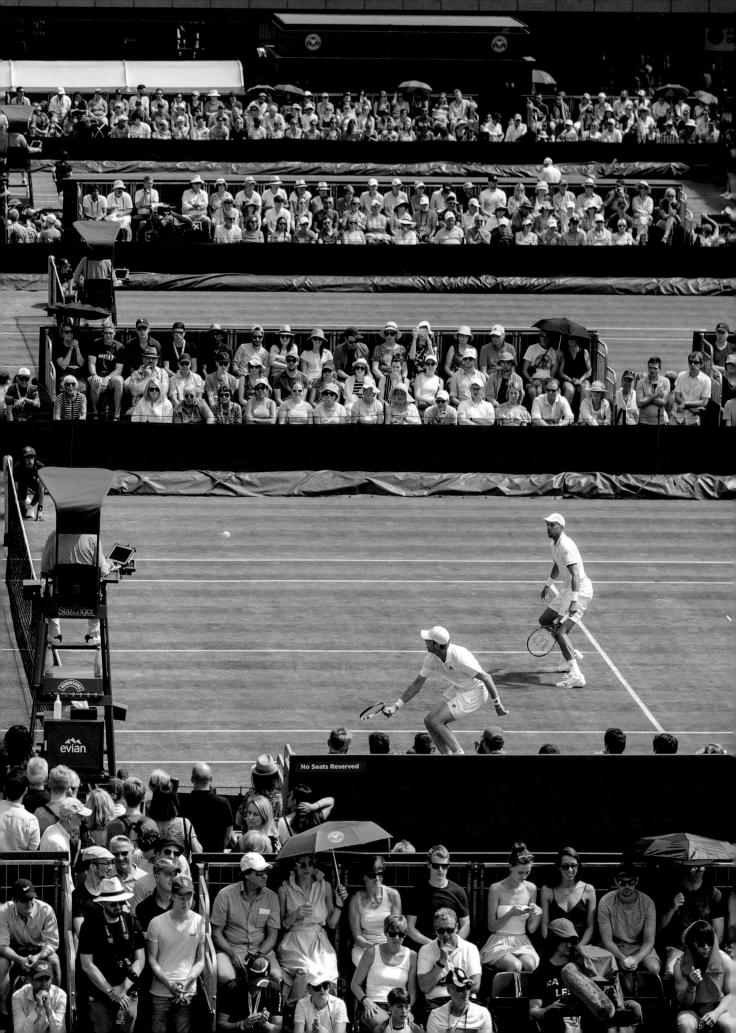

Previous pages: Court 15 saw the big-hitting duo of Gilles Muller and Sam Querrey outduelled over five compelling sets by the Croatian pairing of Nikola Mektic and Franko Skugor

Above: It's one thing playing your hero but quite another beating him, as Adam Pavlasek discovered when Novak Djokovic powered past him to record a clinical victory

Djokovic needed just 94 minutes to complete a 6-2, 6-2, 6-1 victory over the Czech Republic's Adam Pavlasek on No.1 Court, where the Serb's campaign had ended 12 months earlier with defeat to Sam Querrey. As a boy Pavlasek idolised Djokovic. "That makes me look old," Djokovic said with a smile. "But it is definitely very nice to hear that I inspired him."

Djokovic had been on course for a rematch of his memorable 2013 semi-final against Juan Martin del Potro, but the Argentinian was comprehensively outplayed by Ernests Gulbis, who won 6-4, 6-4, 7-6(3). Gulbis had needed a 'protected' world ranking to get into the draw after dropping out of the world's top 500 following a lengthy absence with injuries. "I played really, really great tennis," the Latvian said afterwards. "I served well. I returned well. In my opinion, del Potro is one of the best players. For sure he has one of the best forehands. He's really tough to beat."

An even bigger surprise was provided by Sebastian Ofner, who beat the No.17 seed, Jack Sock, 6-3, 6-4, 3-6, 2-6, 6-2. Ofner, the world No.217, had never played on grass before the qualifying tournament, in which he won three matches to secure his place in the Main Draw of a Grand Slam event for the first time. Having beaten Thomaz Bellucci, the world No.55, in the first round, Ofner claimed an even bigger scalp with his victory over Sock, who had begun the year by winning titles in Auckland and Delray Beach. Ofner nearly trebled his career earnings by guaranteeing himself prize money of at least £90,000 with his run to the third round.

The 21-year-old Austrian is coached by Wolfgang Thiem, whose son, Dominic, reached the third round for the first time with a 5-7, 6-4, 6-2, 6-4 victory over Gilles Simon. Milos Raonic, last year's runner-up, lost the first set before beating Mikhail Youzhny 3-6, 7-6(7), 6-4, 7-5, while Gael Monfils, the No.15 seed, beat Britain's Kyle Edmund 7-6(1), 6-4, 6-4. John Isner, the No.23 seed, hit 45 aces but lost in five sets to Dudi Sela, and Paolo Lorenzi, the No.32 seed, lost in four sets to Jared Donaldson.

Del Potro warms the heart

Not for the first time this summer, Juan Martin del Potro cemented his reputation as one of the game's good guys

• **If not for Rafael Nadal's 10th title triumph** in the French Open, Juan Martin del Potro may well have ended up as the man of the hour at Roland Garros when he earned the plaudits of the entire sporting world for his compassionate consoling of stricken opponent Nicolas Almagro, who was in tears after being forced to pull out of their second round match with a knee injury.

At Wimbledon the popular Argentine once again switched into Good Samaritan mode on a sweltering day while doing battle with Ernests Gulbis on No.3 Court.

The No.29 seed received cheers from the onlooking fans when, recognising a problem in the crowd, he stopped to organise for a bottle of water to be passed up to an elderly lady who was clearly suffering in the heat, while Ball Boys also collected bags of ice to be sent to her and St John Ambulance staff sprang into action.

"We were scared about the situation," del Potro admitted afterwards on a day when this spectator was one of around 60 people who needed treatment in the Grounds for heat-related issues.

• **When John Isner and Dudi Sela take to the court** there's always a splendid little-and-large act guaranteed! As they prepared for their match on Court 12, the two men stood side-by-side at the net for a pre-match photo.

It wasn't the first time the pair had enjoyed this sort of comical photo opportunity, with the 5ft 9in Sela always game for a laugh

The long and the short of it is that John Isner and Dudi Sela always have fun when they do battle. This time, the Israeli ended with the biggest smile

when taking on giant opponents, once even standing on a linesman's chair to give 6ft 11in Ivo Karlovic a hug.

This time it was the 6ft 10in Isner making mischief, unable to resist exacerbating their height difference by stretching as high as possible on tiptoe while Sela tried (and failed...) not to chuckle.

However, it was Sela who was to earn the last laugh, David eventually bringing down the 45-ace Goliath 6-7(5), 7-6(5), 5-7, 7-6(5), 6-3 after almost four hours.

• **Roger Federer's international fan club** was out in red-and-white force on Centre Court to watch their hero defeat Dusan Lajovic, and the prize for the best of the many enterprising tributes to the seven-time champion had to go to the lady seen sporting the badge bearing the legend 'Rogerholics Anonymous'.

DAY
5
FRIDAY
7 JULY

The Queue Section sign reads:

Queue Section

K | 9

THE QUEUE CODE OF CONDUCT

Since Dorothea Lambert Chambers won the last of her seven Wimbledon singles titles in 1914, only one mother has lifted the Venus Rosewater Dish. With Petra Kvitova and Karolina Pliskova, two of the pre-tournament favourites, on their way home, would The Championships 2017 be a chance for Victoria Azarenka to emulate Evonne Cawley, who won the title in 1980, three years after the birth of her first child?

Previous pages: A view across the Grounds from the top of No.3 Court takes in some of The Championships' world-famous flora

Above: The Queue, one of Wimbledon's great traditions, was as popular as ever, especially with the lovely weather tempting a host of newcomers to SW19

Azarenka returned to competition at the Mallorca Open a fortnight before the start of The Championships and just six months after the birth of her son, Leo. The two-time Australian Open champion and former world No.1 had often performed well at the All England Club and reached the semi-finals in 2011 and 2012, both times losing to the eventual champions, Kvitova and Serena Williams respectively.

The Belarusian proved she had lost none of her competitive spirit when she saved three match points in beating Japan's Risa Ozaki in her first comeback match in Mallorca and then came from a set down to beat Catherine Bellis in the first round at The Championships. A straight-sets victory over Elena Vesnina, the No.15 seed and 2016 semi-finalist, underlined Azarenka's undoubted quality and set up an intriguing third round meeting with Britain's Heather Watson in day five's opening match on Centre Court.

Watson, who was on her own comeback trail after dropping out of the world's top 100, was playing her first singles match on Centre Court since her remarkable third round encounter with Williams two years earlier, when she had gone within two points of beating the then world No.1. On another day of glorious sunshine, which saw the Centre Court roof closed in the morning to protect the grass from the heat before being reopened before the start of play, Watson made a fine start. However, after the Briton had broken serve at the first attempt and taken the first set in just 34 minutes, the momentum shifted as Azarenka turned up the power to level the match. Watson, who has never reached the second week at a Grand Slam tournament, fought ferociously to stay in the deciding set but at 4-4 Azarenka made the decisive break and went on to serve out for a 3-6, 6-1, 6-4 victory.

"I felt that the match at the end there could have gone either way," Watson said afterwards. "We had a lot of long rallies and games that went back and forth, but Vika played great. I thought she got better and better as the match went on. She just kept applying pressure."

Azarenka preferred to describe her return as "a new chapter in my life" rather than a comeback. "It's like a second career," she said. "I feel like whatever happened in the past is really in the past. I have those achievements and all those titles, but now I feel like a new me in a way."

Wimbledon, like the three other Grand Slam tournaments, provides creche facilities, which Azarenka would like to see at every event on the Women's Tennis Association tour. "I'll do anything to make that happen, because I think it's really important," she said.

Watson, who later joined forces with Henri Kontinen to beat Azarenka and Nenad Zimonjic in a successful start to the defence of their mixed doubles title, had been one of four Britons through to the third round of singles. However, by the end of the day only two were left standing. Aljaz Bedene's hopes of reaching the second week of a Grand Slam tournament for the first time were dashed by Gilles Muller, who beat him on grass for the second time in a month. Muller won 7-6(4), 7-5, 6-4, though the fact that the match took nearly two-and-a-half hours was an indication of how tight it had been.

Victoria Azarenka's return (**below left**) to Wimbledon gathered further momentum as the powers of the player dubbed 'Supermum' by the media proved too much for home favourite Heather Watson (**below right**)

The defeats of Kvitova and Pliskova had left Johanna Konta as the favourite to win the ladies' singles, but if the 26-year-old Briton felt any extra pressure there was no sign of it as she brushed aside Greece's Maria Sakkari 6-4, 6-1 in just 76 minutes on No.1 Court. "Everyone in the draw is in with a chance of taking the title," Konta said when asked how it felt to be tipped for success. "Favourites also come and go. They change daily, almost. I'm just here, happy to have actually made it into the second week, happy to come through three battles this week. I'm very much taking it one match at a time, but I'm definitely working towards staying involved for a full two weeks."

While Konta reached the fourth round for the first time, Andy Murray booked his place in it for the 10th year in a row with a battling 6-2, 4-6, 6-1, 7-5 victory over Fabio Fognini on Centre Court. In a fascinating match of rapidly changing fortunes, Murray trailed 5-2 in the fourth set before showing his customary grit to break the will of the No.28 seed, who had played one of his best matches on grass. Indeed, Fognini said afterwards that he had been the better player for most of the match.

Murray took the first set in just 29 minutes, Fognini dropping his serve in the final game after three successive double faults. The volatile Italian played much better in the second set, only for his level to dip in the third, during which he lost a game after being deducted a point for a second code violation. With the evening light starting to fade as Fognini went 5-2 up in the fourth set it seemed likely that the match would have to be halted to allow the roof to be closed for a decider.

However, on a day when Murray's brother Jamie and his partner Bruno Soares lost to Sam Groth and Robert Lindstedt in the gentlemen's doubles, the world No.1 fought back with a typically gutsy rearguard action. Murray saved five set points over the next three games, one of them after Fognini stopped playing in order to contest a line call, having forgotten that he had run out of challenges. At 5-5 Fognini dropped serve for the seventh time, after which Murray served out for victory with his 15th ace.

"The match was pretty up and down from both of us," Murray said afterwards. "I didn't feel like I played my best tennis, but I won and I got through it." When asked how his sore hip had been, Murray admitted that he had not moved as well as he had in his first two matches, though he did not think he would have had any problems playing a fifth set.

If Murray's form was patchy the same could not be said of Rafael Nadal's. The former champion faced a potentially tricky encounter with the big-hitting Karen Khachanov. Nadal, however, was on his game from the start and won 6-1, 6-4, 7-6(3) with a typically swashbuckling display. Khachanov played better in the latter stages, but by then the damage was done. "For a set and a half I was playing fantastic," Nadal said afterwards. Khachanov agreed. "At the beginning he started really fast," the 21-year-old Russian said. "He was destroying me."

RALLYING ROUND BETHANIE

The tennis world was quick to show its support for Bethanie Mattek-Sands as the American recovered in a Wimbledon hospital following a shocking fall the previous day that left her in agony and suffering from a ruptured patellar tendon.

Moved by the plight of his 32-year-old compatriot, Jack Sock – who won Olympic gold for the USA with Mattek-Sands in the mixed doubles in Rio de Janeiro the previous year – led the tributes from her friends and colleagues.

Sock wrote out his friend's name in marker pen on his trainers – which he wore in his mixed doubles match partnering Madison Keys – and posted a picture of them on Twitter with the message: "Wearing these on court for you today @BMATTEK."

Fans around the world and other fellow professionals swiftly inundated the popular American with messages of goodwill. Her best friend Lucie Safarova, who had been in line to shoot for a sixth Grand Slam title with Mattek-Sands in the ladies' doubles, had been left in tears herself at courtside when the injury occurred and later wrote on Instagram: "She is the biggest fighter and one of the strongest people I know! I hope to see that great smile on court again soon!" Meanwhile the great Martina Navratilova echoed the thoughts of everyone by tweeting: "Am just devastated about Bethanie Mattek-Sands and her injury – we are all behind you, hoping for the best."

As for the patient herself, she reckoned she felt quite buoyed by everyone rallying around her. "All your messages have been really inspiring and have meant a lot to me," Mattek-Sands said. "The support has been amazing. I'll get through this."

The injury to Bethanie Mattek-Sands, pictured here in practice prior to The Championships, provoked a heartwarming outpouring of support from the tennis community

Roberto Bautista Agut, the No.18 seed, reached the fourth round for the seventh time in the last nine Grand Slam tournaments when he beat the No.9 seed, Kei Nishikori, 6-4, 7-6(3), 3-6, 6-3. Nishikori, who had been in patchy form after a spate of injuries, said he had found it hard to find any sort of rhythm. Marin Cilic made only 13 unforced errors in an emphatic 6-4, 7-6(3), 6-4 victory over Steve Johnson, who was in tears during the third set following the recent death of his father. Sam Querrey was leading Jo-Wilfried Tsonga 6-5 in the final set when their superb match was suspended because of darkness.

Dominika Cibulkova, the No.8 seed, was the most significant loser in the ladies' singles, going down 6-7(3), 6-3, 4-6 to the 19-year-old Croatian, Ana Konjuh, who reached the fourth round for the first time. Camila Giorgi had her chances against Jelena Ostapenko, the French Open champion, but lost 5-7, 5-7 after squandering a 5-3 lead in the first set and a 5-2 lead in the second. The No.2 seed, Simona Halep, who lost to Ostapenko in the final at Roland Garros, saved a set point in the second set before beating Peng Shuai 6-4, 7-6(7).

Naomi Osaka, a 19-year-old Japanese with an explosive game, faced one of her childhood idols when she took on Venus Williams and pushed the five-time champion hard before losing 6-7(3), 4-6. Osaka, who was not born when 37-year-old Williams made her debut at The Championships, led 3-0 in the tie-break but then lost seven points in a row. The world No.59, who has a Japanese mother and a Haitian father, hit more aces and winners than Williams and struck the fastest serve of the match at 120mph. "She deserved to win," Williams said afterwards. "She played an amazing match today."

Japanese teenager Naomi Osaka gave 37-year-old Venus Williams a real fight in their 'generation game' before finally succumbing to the five-time champion

1 2 3
4 5 6

Never give up

Now you see him, now you don't! Joe Salisbury pulled off a magic trick to play perhaps the shot of The Championships

● **Could there have been a more extraordinary point** won at The Championships than that conjured up by British player Joe Salisbury while partnering Katy Dunne against Neal Skupski and Anna Smith in their mixed doubles contest on Court 12?

In the second set, the 25-year-old couldn't stop his momentum from carrying him headlong towards the courtside seats as he desperately attempted to retrieve a seemingly decisive smash. Yet not only did Salisbury hurdle the fence into the seats but he also managed to loft the ball back into play before bounding back on to the court and volleying a backhand winner.

Sensational stuff, but his heroics couldn't prevent him from ending up on the losing team.

● **If you've got the Masters green jacket**, then flaunt it! Luminaries from the world of sport traditionally take centre stage on the first Saturday of The Championships but Spanish golfing superstar Sergio Garcia headed a distinguished list of sporting greats – including footballer David Beckham and All Blacks rugby legend Dan Carter – who turned up a day early in 2017.

Garcia was resplendent in the prize he won at Augusta in April as he watched his friend and compatriot Rafael Nadal beat Karen Khachanov on Centre Court and was also invited to join Roberto Bautista Agut's team in the No.3 Court box to see the Spaniard defeat Kei Nishikori.

Masters champions like nothing more than wearing their hallowed green jacket at Wimbledon. A year after Danny Willett paraded his prize, a proud Sergio Garcia followed suit

● **There was a happy ending** to a strange saga as a teenage fan of Jack Sock got to meet his hero and was presented with a Wimbledon towel by the big-hearted American.

Three days earlier Peter Woodville, a 14-year-old from Philadelphia, received widespread sympathy after an older fan – who should have known better – ripped from his grasp a towel that Sock had thrown into the crowd after his first round victory over Christian Garin.

Shocked when he saw footage of the incident, Sock made efforts to track down the youngster and give him a replacement, finally meeting up with him after his first round mixed doubles match. As he handed Peter the prized towel, the No.17 seed shook his hand and told him "really sorry, buddy". All's well that ends well...

DAY
6

SATURDAY
8 JULY

T he sporting superstars in the Royal Box on day six would no doubt have recognised the moment when Novak Djokovic demonstrated that the fire which had driven him to so much success in the past had been well and truly reignited.

Previous pages: The first Saturday was, as ever, a serious working day at Wimbledon when the real title hopefuls, like Novak Djokovic, all had to knuckle down to ensure they were still standing for the second week

Above: Djokovic recognised how dangerous the mercurial Latvian Ernests Gulbis can be and thus was in a no-nonsense mood on Centre Court

There had been moments in the previous 13 months when the Serb seemed to some observers to be in the midst of a long-term decline, but in the second game of his third round meeting with Ernests Gulbis it was clear that the 2015 Gentlemen's Singles champion's intensity was well and truly back. "That's two points in a row," Djokovic barked at Jake Garner after two debatable decisions by the umpire. "Focus, please!"

After completing an emphatic 6-4, 6-1, 7-6(2) victory Djokovic apologised for his heat-of-the-moment outburst, but there were other times, too, when his emotions rose to the surface as he celebrated important points with roars of approval. Djokovic's former coach, Boris Becker, commentating on the BBC, suggested that the No.2 seed's combative mood was an indication that he was recapturing the passion that had taken him to 12 Grand Slam titles. "Boris knows me very well," Djokovic said later. "He's right when he says that the passion is back. I've been feeling better on the court."

On the equivalent day at last year's Championships Djokovic had suffered a defeat that proved to be a sign of what lay ahead. He had arrived at the All England Club as the first man to hold all four Grand Slam singles titles for 47 years, but his run of 28 consecutive appearances in Grand Slam quarter-finals was ended in the third round by Sam Querrey. As his form continued to falter, Djokovic lost his world No.1 position to Andy Murray at the end of the year and dropped to No.4 in the rankings – his lowest position since 2009 – after a lacklustre defeat to Dominic Thiem in the quarter-finals of the 2017 French Open.

Unusual circumstances call for unusual measures and Djokovic responded to his decline by dismissing his entire coaching team and then persuading Andre Agassi to help him, with Mario Ancic also joining his entourage at The Championships. Come the grass court season, Djokovic played a warm-up tournament before Wimbledon for the first time in seven years and was rewarded with the title at Eastbourne. By the time he had beaten Gulbis he was on his longest winning run – seven matches – since the previous year's French Open.

Gulbis, having dropped out of the world's top 500 after a series of injuries, had found much of his old form to defeat Juan Martin del Potro in the previous round. He raced into a 4-2 lead against Djokovic, but the Serb then won nine games in a row to take a grip on the match. Djokovic's total of just 12 unforced errors was a stark reminder of the consistency that had taken him to so much success in the past. "Obviously when you're playing well, then you're feeling well, then you're even more motivated, passionate to see how far it can take you," Djokovic said after reaching the second week of The Championships for the tenth time.

If Djokovic's record at Wimbledon was impressive, how about Roger Federer's? The seven-time champion was aiming to reach the fourth round for the 15th time and did so with a 7-6(3), 6-4, 6-4 victory over Mischa Zverev. It meant that the 35-year-old Swiss had made the second week in 48 of his last 50 Grand Slam tournaments, having missed out only at The Championships in 2013 and at the Australian Open in 2015. By the end of the day Federer was one of a record seven men aged 30 or over through to the fourth round.

Mischa and Alexander Zverev were the first brothers to be seeded at The Championships since Sandy and Gene Mayer in 1982. While 20-year-old Alexander is one of the most exciting players of his generation, 29-year-old Mischa had spent much of his career on the Challenger circuit until his fortunes picked up at the end of 2016. He enjoyed the biggest win of his career when he beat Andy Murray at the 2017 Australian Open.

Gulbis had been looking like his old self again after suffering injuries to his back, shoulder, calf and right wrist over the last two seasons, but Djokovic proved a hurdle too far

THE GOLDEN GENERATION

The tradition of top British sportsmen and women gracing the Royal Box on the first Saturday was maintained in 2017 with no less than 37 of Team GB's Olympic and Paralympic champions from the 2016 Rio de Janeiro Games being invited to SW19.

It was marvellous to see gold medallists from 10 different sports all taking a bow, but it was the surprise appearance of the Olympic tennis champion himself that ensured a certain Andy Murray perhaps stole the show on his favourite stage.

Murray, who had won the 2012 Olympic crown on Centre Court and successfully defended the title in Rio, prompted the biggest round of applause as he walked down the stairs of the box and was introduced to the crowd by Sue Barker. It was later pointed out that in wearing a white tracksuit for his brief appearance the 30-year-old Scot was technically in violation of the strict Royal Box dress code, but our busy champion had actually been given special dispensation after rushing over from the practice courts to be part of the ceremony.

Clockwise from top: the Royal Box dress code was waived just this once for Scotland's finest; Paralympic swimmer Stephanie Millward displays her two gold medals; Jason and Laura Kenny, the first couple of British cycling with 10 Olympic golds between them, wave to the crowd

Gold medallists all! Top: Rowers Scott Durant, Peter Reed, Matt Gotrel, Tom Ransley, cox Phelan Hill (partially obscured behind Triggs Hodge) and Andrew Triggs Hodge, members of the triumphant men's eight. Middle row: Hockey stars Hannah Macleod, Georgie Twigg, Crista Cullen and Kate Richardson-Walsh; Victorious Paralympic sprinters Libby Clegg and Georgina Hermitage; Joe Clarke, winner in the K1 canoe slalom. Left: World record-breaking swimmer Adam Peaty; eight-time Paralympic equestrian champion Sophie Christiansen; Giles Scott, sailor, winner in the Finn class

The elder Zverev is one of a dying breed in that serve-and-volley is his default mode. The German was expected to pose Federer some problems, but as he charged into the net he ran into a barrage of passing shots. The first set was close, but Federer did not have to defend any break points thereafter and eventually closed out victory after an hour and 49 minutes, having yet to drop a set in the tournament.

While Mischa Zverev was still waiting to reach the fourth round 10 years after his debut at The Championships, his younger brother made it at only the third attempt. Alexander booked his passage with a resounding 6-4, 6-4, 6-2 victory over Sebastian Ofner. Milos Raonic, the previous year's runner-up, and Tomas Berdych also won with something to spare, beating Albert Ramos-Vinolas and David Ferrer respectively, while Thiem reached the second week for the fourth Grand Slam tournament in a row by beating Jared Donaldson 7-5, 6-4, 6-2.

The number of retirements from the gentlemen's singles rose to nine when Dudi Sela quit with an injury after going two sets down to Grigor Dimitrov, while Querrey needed just four minutes and 15 seconds to complete his victory over Jo-Wilfried Tsonga, their match having been suspended because of fading light the previous evening with the American leading in the final set.

Angelique Kerber's frustrating form continued as the world No.1 had to come from a set and 4-2 down to beat Shelby Rogers, the world No.70. Rogers, who attacked from the start, hit 48 winners to Kerber's 25, though in the end the more telling statistics were the 24-year-old American's 47 unforced errors compared with the 29-year-old German's 14. "She was hitting the balls very hard," Kerber said after her 4-6, 7-6(2), 6-4 victory. "In the end I think the key was that I was fighting and never gave up, no matter what the score was."

Agnieszka Radwanska and Caroline Wozniacki also came from behind before securing their places in the second week. Radwanska, the runner-up in 2012, beat Timea Bacsinszky 3-6, 6-4, 6-1, but only after her opponent picked up a thigh injury in the second set which led to her taking a medical time-out. With her thigh heavily strapped Bacsinszky lost power on her groundstrokes, though Radwanska felt the match had turned thanks to her own increased aggression in the second set.

Opposite: Caroline Wozniacki raises her arms in delight on No.1 Court after prevailing in a tremendous three-set scrap with rising Estonian star Anett Kontaveit, who had served twice for the match in the second set

Below: Alexander Zverev, Germany's exciting young star, made it into the second week of a Grand Slam for the first time with his 6-4, 6-4, 6-2 win over Austrian qualifier Sebastian Ofner on No.2 Court

Wozniacki went even closer to defeat against Anett Kontaveit, who had been within two points of victory before losing 6-3, 6-7(3), 2-6. Kontaveit, who had claimed her first title in the 's-Hertogenbosch grass court tournament the previous month, was serving at 5-4 and 30-0 in the second set when she missed what should have been a simple backhand. The 21-year-old Estonian dropped her serve, broke back immediately, but then failed to serve out for victory for a second time, after which Wozniacki took control. "I'm just happy I survived today," Wozniacki said afterwards. "I fought. I didn't give up."

Garbiñe Muguruza, the No.14 seed, had no such problems against Sorana Cirstea, winning 6-2, 6-2 in just 70 minutes. However, despite not dropping a set in any of the first three rounds, the 2015 runner-up admitted that she still had trouble adapting to grass. "I never feel that comfortable on grass," Muguruza said. "Every time I start the grass season, I'm like, 'How the hell did I reach that final?' The experience I have playing matches for now helps me, for sure, but it's tough. Everybody knows it's tough."

CoCo Vandeweghe was an equally convincing winner, beating her fellow American, Alison Riske, 6-2, 6-4 to make the fourth round for the third year in a row. The No.24 seed, who reached the semi-finals of the Australian Open in January, had a clear advantage in terms of power, hitting seven aces and 23 winners. After parting company with her coach, Craig Kardon, in the build-up to The Championships, Vandeweghe sought the assistance of Pat Cash and said the Australian had made "a pretty big impact" in the short time they had been working together.

Marcus Willis, a headline-maker at The Championships 12 months previously, turned the world rankings on their head again when he teamed up with his fellow Briton, Jay Clarke, to beat the defending champions, Nicolas Mahut and Pierre-Hugues Herbert, 3-6, 6-1, 7-6(3), 5-7, 6-3 in the second round of the gentlemen's doubles. The previous year, ranked No.722

in the world, Willis had won three matches in qualifying to reach the Main Draw of the singles, in which he lost to Federer in the second round. This time he fell in the final round of qualifying but was given a wild card into the doubles with 18-year-old Clarke.

Willis (world No.708 in doubles) and Clarke (No.882) came back from two sets down to win their opening match against Donaldson and Jeevan Nedunchezhiyan and surpassed that performance with a remarkable victory over Mahut and Herbert in front of a boisterous crowd on No.3 Court. The Britons appeared to have blown their chances after losing eight points in a row when Herbert served at 4-5 and 0-40 in the fourth set, but served out for the decider after making an early break. Bob and Mike Bryan, three-time Wimbledon champions, also went out, losing 3-6, 5-7, 4-6 to Marcin Matkowski and Max Mirnyi, who at 40 was one year older than the American twins.

The house is on fire

There were no alarms for Garbiñe Muguruza against Sorana Cirstea on No.2 Court, which is more than could be said for the Spaniard back in the kitchen of her Wimbledon house…

• **Garbiñe Muguruza only allowed Sorana Cirstea** four games in their third round match, and afterwards revealed that her smoking hot run of form wasn't just limited to the tennis court…

Spain's 2015 ladies' singles finalist explained she'd already had a few adventures at her rented Wimbledon home but nothing quite as alarming as when she attempted to cook herself a steak on the eve of her clash with Cirstea.

"It was so much smoke… the fire alarm was, like, under where you cook. I'm like, 'Why do you put a fire alarm there?'" she smiled, adding that the alarm rang for about 20 minutes until it finally stopped. She even posted a video online of herself and her coaching adviser Conchita Martinez wafting pillows and opening windows in a bid to ensure the fire brigade didn't make an unnecessary trip.

• **Muguruza's was not the only internet hit** to emerge from SW19 featuring a Spanish star, as a video of Rafael Nadal shopping at a Tesco Express in Wimbledon and bravely struggling to work out how to use the self-service checkout became an instant worldwide sensation. The Twitter user who was amazed to find himself helping Rafa work it out summed his feelings up perfectly in a simple tweet: "Surreal."

• **Caroline Wozniacki, one of Serena Williams' closest friends** on the circuit, revealed that she was hoping for a job with the champion – as her babysitter!

By the sound of it, though, the great Dane's sweet tooth could have been a bit of a problem in her audition to be 'Auntie Caro'.

"I think I'm a great babysitter," said Wozniacki after her third round win over Anett Kontaveit, "but I'm not sure Serena agrees! She has told me already some set rules that I'm not allowed to break. I usually have candy around the house. That's not allowed any more. I'm trying to follow her rules, but we'll see…"

• **By the first Saturday the Competitors' Restaurant** is at its busiest and, as usual, trade was roaring as the assembled stars hungrily took advantage of the 3,000 kilos of bananas, 28,000 kilos of strawberries and a daily mountain of 80 to 90 kilos of fresh pasta that had been ordered.

Yet whereas in previous years pasta was the preferred fuel of champions, now the popular sushi bar seemed to have taken over with many players deeply impressed with how the treat aids muscle recovery.

Sushi and strawberries: fuelling today's Wimbledon players

And the outstanding sushi chomper? Well, big John Isner was reported to have ordered no less than 36 salmon nigiri rolls on one particular evening…

DAY
7
MONDAY
10 JULY

Within minutes of winning his tenth French Open title Rafael Nadal had cast doubts on his chances at The Championships, saying that for the last five years his troublesome knees had prevented him from playing at his best on grass. The last time the 31-year-old Spaniard had gone beyond the fourth round was in 2011.

Previous pages: A huge crowd gathered on The Hill, enthralled by the epic contest between Rafa Nadal and Gilles Muller as it unfolded on No.1 Court in the shimmering evening sunshine

Above: Nadal saved four match points in a marathon final set but, after a monumental tussle, it proved in vain for the 15-time Grand Slam champion

However, after three successive straight-sets victories, Nadal's supporters were daring to dream that a third Wimbledon title might be on the cards. After all, Nadal had just won the French Open without dropping a set for the third time; on the two previous occasions he had done so, in 2008 and 2010, he had gone on to triumph at Wimbledon.

'Manic Monday', when all the remaining players in the gentlemen's and ladies' singles are scheduled to play, saw Nadal paired with the No.16 seed, Gilles Muller, a 34-year-old from Luxembourg enjoying an Indian summer to his career. Seeded at The Championships for the first time, the big-serving left-hander was at a lifetime-best position of No.26 in the world rankings having won the only titles of his career in the preceding six months, on hard courts in Sydney and on grass at 's-Hertogenbosch. The two men had met at Wimbledon on two previous occasions, Muller winning in the second round in 2005 and Nadal in the third in 2011.

What followed was one of the most thrilling matches of The Championships 2017, Muller winning 6-3, 6-4, 3-6, 4-6, 15-13 after four hours and 48 minutes of high drama on No.1 Court. While Muller had the edge in serving power, hitting 30 aces to Nadal's 23, and cracked 95 winners to the Spaniard's 77, the former champion hit his groundstrokes more consistently and covered the court to better effect. Nadal also won more points – 198 to Muller's 191.

In the first two sets there were only six break points, Muller converting two of his three and successfully defending all three of Nadal's. The momentum swung as Nadal took the third and fourth sets, but for most of the decider – which lasted two-and-a-quarter hours – there was nothing to choose between the two men. Nadal saved two match points at 4-5 and two more at 9-10, while Muller held firm at 6-6, when he saved one break point, and at 9-9, when he saved four more. Having held serve to stay in the match nine times, Nadal finally succumbed at 13-14. "Most of the time in the fifth set he played more aggressively and he played better than me," a typically magnanimous Nadal said afterwards. Muller said it had been "a big battle" and was "just glad it's over".

It was a day for five-set marathons. Milos Raonic and Tomas Berdych held back the new generation, the Canadian beating Alexander Zverev 4-6, 7-5, 4-6, 7-5, 6-1 and the Czech winning a see-saw contest with Dominic Thiem 6-3, 6-7(1), 6-3, 3-6, 6-3. Sam Querrey won a battle of the big servers, beating Kevin Anderson 5-7, 7-6(5), 6-3, 6-7(11), 6-3.

Marin Cilic continued his impressive progress, crushing Roberto Bautista Agut 6-2, 6-2, 6-2 to reach the quarter-finals for the fourth year in a row, while Roger Federer won a meeting of two great stylists, beating Grigor Dimitrov 6-4, 6-2, 6-4. In his early days Dimitrov was nicknamed 'Baby Fed' in recognition of the similarities of his game to Federer's. The 26-year-old Bulgarian, a semi-finalist in 2014, has developed into a fine player in his own right, but Federer, who had yet to drop a set in the tournament, eased into the quarter-finals for the 15th time, an Open era record.

After four hours and 48 minutes of magnificent fare that took us late into the evening, Luxembourger Muller finally eked out probably the finest win of his long career

While still hobbling between points, Andy Murray felt he was moving better and hitting the ball cleaner than in his third round struggle against Fabio Fognini as he defeated France's Benoit Paire in straight sets

Andy Murray, meanwhile, continued to dispense with some of the game's more flamboyant characters as Benoit Paire went the way of Alexander Bublik, Dustin Brown and Fabio Fognini. The world No.1's 7-6(1), 6-4, 6-4 victory was his 28th in succession against Frenchmen in Grand Slam competition. It took him into his 10th Wimbledon quarter-final, a record bettered in the Open era only by Federer, Jimmy Connors and Boris Becker.

Paire, who was attempting to reach his first Grand Slam singles quarter-final, played with his customary flair but went for too many drop shots and had his erratic forehand regularly exposed. The world No.46 likes to run round his forehand to hit his preferred backhand instead, but Murray was all too aware of the tactic. "I thought I played well," the defending champion said afterwards. "That was by far the best I've hit the ball so far in the tournament."

Murray's win followed Johanna Konta's 7-6(3), 4-6, 6-4 victory over Caroline Garcia, which meant that Britain would have a man and a woman in the quarter-finals for the first time since Roger Taylor and Virginia Wade in 1973. Konta became the first home player to reach the last eight of the ladies' singles since Jo Durie in 1984.

Konta's victory in a contest between two big-hitting baseliners was important in that her defeat to Garcia at Indian Wells in March had been the only time her coach, Wim Fissette, had seen her falter mentally as she lost a deciding tie-break 1-7. On this occasion Konta stayed strong, even if there were times when she was outhit. The Briton failed to serve out for the opening set at 5-4 but dominated the tie-break before Garcia won five games in a row to take charge of the second set. There was only one break point in the decider, which Konta converted at 4-4 when Garcia missed a forehand. "It was such a tough match to play," Konta said afterwards. "It's hard to get any rhythm when she's serving so well and gets her first strike in."

No. 1 Court Queue

Centre Court Queue

JUST THE TICKET

Wimbledon's Ticket Resale scheme had already raised £2.5 million for charitable causes since its introduction in 1954, and The Championships 2017 – blessed by huge crowds like the one that flocked to Manic Monday's exciting programme – provided more substantial funds that will be put towards worthy causes.

The ever-popular system allows spectators already in the Grounds to buy returned Show Court tickets after 3pm from the Ticket Resale Kiosk north of Court 18 near the top of St Mary's Walk.

Centre Court and No.1 Court tickets are resold at £10 and No.2 Court tickets are available for £5, with all the proceeds distributed to charity through the Wimbledon Foundation.

In all, a total of £173,212.50 was raised in 2017 but that was doubled to £346,425 after Official Suppliers HSBC generously matched that figure to help celebrate the 63rd anniversary of the scheme.

As usual, local charities and the armed forces benefitted, and in light of the terrorist attacks in the capital and Manchester in 2017 as well as the tragic fire at Grenfell Tower in London, funds were also donated to the British Red Cross UK Solidarity Fund and The London Community Foundation's Grenfell Tower Appeal.

WIMBLEDON FOUNDATION

Murray welcomed the success of another British player. "It's important to have various different role models in the sport, players competing for the biggest events," he said. To the surprise of most attending his post-match media conference, the Scot added: "I do think it makes a difference to the interest in the sport, because a lot of people who follow tennis in this country won't enjoy watching me play."

With so many top players in action, this was an excellent day for spectators on all of the Show Courts. No.2 Court witnessed one of the matches of the Fortnight as Garbiñe Muguruza beat Angelique Kerber 4-6, 6-4, 6-4 in a captivating contrast of styles. While Kerber's strengths are her athleticism and defence, Muguruza is an aggressive stroke-maker who appreciates the importance of attacking the net and has grown increasingly confident with her volleys.

The first two sets were decided by single breaks of serve, but in the decider the advantage swung one way and then the other. At 3-3 Muguruza saved four break points before Kerber, serving at 4-5, saved two match points with some bold attacking play before the Spaniard took her third opportunity thanks to a decisive return. Kerber's defeat meant that she would lose the world No.1 ranking at the end of The Championships to either Simona Halep or Karolina Pliskova.

Halep stayed in contention for both the world No.1 position and her first Grand Slam title by ending Victoria Azarenka's run. The two-time Australian Open champion dominated for periods of the first set but faded in the tie-break and was overwhelmed in the second set as Halep won 7-6(3), 6-2. Azarenka was disappointed with her performance but said that being able to return to baby Leo afterwards made a difference. "I don't go back to an empty house after my loss and just cry there," she said. "I go home and spend time with my son. Regardless of whether I've won or lost, he's still going to smile when he sees me."

Svetlana Kuznetsova reached her first Wimbledon singles quarter-final for 10 years by beating Agnieszka Radwanska 6-2, 6-4 while Magdalena Rybarikova continued her run with a 6-4, 2-6, 6-3 victory over Petra Martic, who had enjoyed a Wimbledon to savour after battling her way through the qualifiers. CoCo Vandeweghe's power proved too much for Caroline Wozniacki, who went down 6-7(4), 4-6, while 37-year-old Venus Williams and 20-year-old Jelena Ostapenko set up an intriguing quarter-final showdown. Williams needed only 63 minutes to beat Ana Konjuh 6-3, 6-2, but Ostapenko met sterner resistance from Elina Svitolina, who saved seven match points before losing 3-6, 6-7(6).

The day's scheduling brought some criticism from players, commentators and the public. The two main Show Courts both featured two gentlemen's singles matches and one from the ladies' singles, meaning that some big names in the latter competition played on smaller courts. Kerber was "really surprised" to find herself playing Muguruza on No.2 Court, while Ostapenko, the French Open champion, thought she deserved to play on a bigger stage than Court 12, pointing out that her opponent, Svitolina, was the world No.4.

Ironically in her defeat against Garbiñe Muguruza Angelique Kerber (**opposite**) looked back to something like her world No.1 best on the very day that she had to surrender the top ranking. 2015 ladies' singles runner-up Muguruza (**above**) eventually prevailed in a high-quality encounter on No.2 Court

Murray suggested that starting earlier than 1pm on Centre Court and No.1 Court might enable an extra ladies' singles match to be scheduled. Richard Lewis, Chief Executive of the All England Club, acknowledged the scheduling challenges that the Second Monday brings with it, but insisted that the daily programme was dictated by "the marquee matches" and had nothing to do with any favouritism of men over women. "You've got this fantastic era for men's tennis," he said. "There have been years where the women have outshone the men, but at the moment it's very hard to argue beyond the big four – Djokovic, Murray, Nadal and Federer – being on Centre Court and No.1 Court." Lewis also pointed out that an earlier start time would present various logistical challenges.

There was also criticism of the fact that Novak Djokovic's match against Adrian Mannarino, which was scheduled as the last on No.1 Court, was not switched to Centre, where play can continue until 11pm under floodlights with the roof closed. Because of the Nadal-Muller marathon, Djokovic and Mannarino never got on court. "The match could not be moved to Centre Court due to the number of spectators remaining in the Grounds," the All England Club said in a statement. "As late as 8.30pm 30,000 people still remained in the Grounds, and therefore moving the match would have created a significant safety issue." At least there should be no such problems come 2019, when No.1 Court's new retractable cover should be in place, the old roof having been removed before The Championships 2017.

Elsewhere, Britain's Marcus Willis and Jay Clarke, who had won their first two matches in the gentlemen's doubles in five sets, bowed out of the competition when they were beaten 3-6, 4-6, 6-7(3) by the No.16 seeds, Oliver Marach and Mate Pavic.

The dark clouds offered the ominous suggestion of a change in the weather but not before Milos Raonic had fought his way past Alexander Zverev to earn a quarter-final with Roger Federer

Mind your head Rafa

Ouch! Rafael Nadal's pre-match mishap caused both Spain's finest and opponent Gilles Muller to chuckle

● **Rafael Nadal provided another of the great social media hits** of The Championships – not to mention quite a hit to his own hard head – while preparing for his epic fourth round match with Gilles Muller.

As the pair were waiting in the tunnel to go out on to No.1 Court, the Spaniard was working himself into the mood for battle with his customary warm-up leaps only to accidentally bash his head into the ceiling with a resounding thud.

It prompted Muller to look around in surprise and the pair both ended up chuckling at the mishap, with the Luxembourger even left to wonder with a grin after his eventual five-set win: "Maybe that's why the first two sets I was winning quite easy! Maybe he was still feeling a little bit dizzy!"

● **Andre Agassi has found life at Wimbledon as a coach** to Novak Djokovic very different to his early days as a player in SW19, back when he was the wildly popular (and at times wildly haired...) idol of countless fans.

"I was always following security guards, never really took it all in," reflected the American, explaining how these days he has been obliged to learn the layout of the Grounds. Indeed, he even ended up having to ask a bystander for directions to Court 10 where his Serbian charge was practising...

● **Jo Konta may have been delighted with her historic progress** towards the quarter-final of the ladies' singles but she was just as happy to oblige reporters hungry for news of the hand-made muffins she bakes for her support team.

"I love to talk about my baking," she laughed. "Today I had white chocolate and raspberry muffins. So far they've been the biggest hit. Previous to that it was a chocolate chip muffin.

"So I'm thinking that maybe tomorrow, if I've got time tonight, it will be a chocolate chip and banana muffin, though I'm getting a lot of pressure to make a banana nut muffin from a certain member of my team. But I'm holding strong..."

Naturally, reporters gobbled up all of this information gleefully...

Johanna Konta came equipped with more than just her racket as she went through security with a smile and a tupperware box. Muffins anyone?

● **Tennis can be a dog's life sometimes.** Svetlana Kuznetsova made her first Wimbledon quarter-final in a decade but she was still pining for an absent and very large friend – her 23-kilo American Bully dog, Dulce. "He's my emotional support animal," the Russian said, adding she has a psychologist's letter explaining why Dulce should travel with her for mental health reasons.

Kuznetsova likes to call her pet on Skype but Venus Williams, who was similarly missing her own pet hound, reckoned she couldn't do that with her Havanese pooch, Harold. "He hears me but doesn't understand where I am... it's too upsetting for him," opined Venus.

ROLEX

KONTA

HALEP

DAY 8

TUESDAY
11 JULY

James Callaghan was in Downing Street, Jimmy Carter was in the White House and John Travolta was in *Grease* the last time Britain had a semi-finalist in the ladies' singles. That player was Virginia Wade who was on Centre Court again, 39 years later, to watch from the Royal Box as Johanna Konta carved out her own place in history.

In 1978 Wade, the defending champion, had beaten Yugoslavia's Mima Jausovec to earn a semi-final meeting with the USA's Chris Evert; now it was Konta's turn to beat an opponent from eastern Europe, Romania's Simona Halep, to secure a semi-final place against another American legend, Venus Williams.

In a Championships that featured many outstanding matches in the ladies' singles, none generated as much excitement and tension as Konta's 6-7(2), 7-6(5), 6-4 victory over Halep. The closed roof over Centre Court, rain having led to the retractable cover being used during matches for the first time in the Fortnight, helped to generate a raucous atmosphere as the home crowd got behind the first British woman to play in the quarter-finals since 1984.

Attacking at every opportunity, Konta struck the ball with great power from the baseline as Halep, arguably the modern game's best all-round athlete, kept forcing her opponent to play the extra shot. The world No.2, who was attempting to reach the semi-finals for the second time, made just nine unforced errors (compared with 36 by Konta) in the 226 points that were contested over more than two-and-a-half hours, while the world No.7 thumped 48 winners (compared with Halep's 26). If the match perhaps lacked the variety of days gone by it more than made up for it with its pulsating rallies. The celebrated coach Nick Bollettieri, writing in *The Independent*, could not recall having witnessed a better women's match in his 60-plus years in the sport.

Konta's unusual service action may not be one for the purists out there but it is wonderfully effective, as she showed in putting 29 of her first 30 first serves in court. Halep had only two break points in the whole match and broke serve just once, in the second game. The opening exchanges were the only time when the occasion seemed to get to Konta, who initially was guilty of over-hitting but was soon striking the ball with her customary controlled aggression. Halep, nevertheless, took command of the first tie-break and in the second was two points away from victory when she served at 5-4, only for Konta to win the next three points with some bold hitting and level the match.

Halep was not happy about the lengthy toilet break Konta took after the second set and when the Romanian dropped serve in the fifth game of the third it became clear that she was not coping well with the pressure. Konta served out for victory, which she secured in unfortunate circumstances when Halep stopped playing on match point after a spectator screamed. Kader Nouni, the umpire, refused to replay the point.

Simona Halep would have become the world No.1 if she had beaten her British rival but, as at the 2017 French Open, the big prize ended up just eluding her

JO FOLLOWS IN VIRGINIA'S FOOTSTEPS

Forty years since she was presented with the Venus Rosewater Dish by Her Majesty Queen Elizabeth II, the 1977 Ladies' Singles champion Virginia Wade was AELTC Chairman Philip Brook's special guest on Centre Court, hoping to see her status as the last British woman to win the trophy ended as she cheered on Johanna Konta's bid to make the semi-finals.

And the 72-year-old, one of the rare few who has a statue of herself at the All England Club, very much liked what she saw from her vantage point in the Royal Box. After Konta had produced a bravura performance, full of fight, resilience and the courage to go for every one of her 48 winners, Wade said: "I'm ultra-impressed. I haven't seen a player with the same sort of dedication and determination for a long time.

"It was absolutely a stunning performance and the pressure was relentless that Konta kept applying. She never really wavered one little bit."

As for potentially losing that tag of 'last champion', Wade confessed she would be perfectly happy. "It's fine to be the last British women's winner of Wimbledon," she smiled, "but it's better to have plenty of British players win."

The result meant that Karolina Pliskova, rather than Halep, would replace Angelique Kerber as world No.1. However, Halep was probably more concerned with the way she had faded in the closing stages. Only a month earlier she had let slip a winning lead against Jelena Ostapenko in the French Open final.

Konta, meanwhile, was assured of becoming only the fourth British woman – after Wade, Sue Barker and Jo Durie – to enter the world's top five since the women's rankings were launched in 1975. "I think the level of tennis that both of us played today, it was just a tremendous match," Konta said afterwards. "To be in the semi-finals of my home Slam, and to do that in front of a full Centre Court, it's pretty, pretty special."

The other quarter-final in the bottom half of the draw brought together, for the first time, 37-year-old Williams and 20-year-old Ostapenko, who had not been born when the five-time Wimbledon champion made her Grand Slam debut at the French Open in 1997. Williams' excellent first six months of 2017 had been crowned by her run to the Australian Open final, while Ostapenko had enjoyed a stunning victory at the French Open. The world No.47, who had never previously won a match at Roland Garros, played all-out attacking tennis from the start to become the first unseeded woman to win in Paris since 1933 and the first woman to secure her maiden tour-level title at a Grand Slam event for 38 years.

The Latvian's all-or-nothing style is perhaps actually better suited to grass than to clay, as she had shown by winning the Wimbledon girls' singles title in 2014, though she subsequently won only one match in her first two appearances in the Main Draw, in 2015 and 2016. Nevertheless, in winning her first four matches this time she had become only the second reigning French Open women's champion in 10 years (after Serena Williams in 2015) to reach the quarter-finals.

Venus Williams ended up commiserating with another youngster at the net after adding 20-year-old French Open champion Jelena Ostapenko (**top**) to her list of beaten opponents at The Championships 2017, which also featured two 19-year-olds in Naomi Osaka and Ana Konjuh

No damp spirits on Konta Cliff

If you wanted to get an idea of quite how completely Wimbledon had fallen for Johanna Konta you didn't need to be under the Centre Court roof, where the British No.1's win over Simona Halep was greeted by the most cacophonous din of the Fortnight. Because outside, wrapped up in their waterproofs and huddled under umbrellas, Konta's ever-increasing fan club filled the air with their cries of 'Go Jo!' and 'C'mon Jo!' just as ecstatically as they watched the Big Screen.

Indeed, it was such a grand occasion – despite the rain – that for an afternoon this wasn't Henman Hill nor Murray Mound but, unquestionably, Konta Cliff.

On her Centre Court debut, however, Ostapenko seemed to lose some of her usual verve, which enabled Williams to take an early grip on the match. The American was soon 3-0 up and took the opening set in just 29 minutes. Ostapenko retrieved an early break in the second set and was within two points of levelling the match when Williams served at 4-5 and 15-30, but the world No.11 hit an ace and was then grateful to see her opponent miss two forehands. Ostapenko was broken in the following game, upon which Williams served out to become the oldest semi-finalist in the ladies' singles for 23 years.

Williams, who was fined $7,500 (about £5,800) for not completing her two mandatory post-match TV interviews after her victory, said at her post-match media conference that she missed her sister, Serena, and their father, Richard, but added: "They're definitely here with me. That is one thing I do know. They're fighting right alongside me."

Garbiñe Muguruza's most recent French Open experience had been rather different to Ostapenko's as the champion of 2016 had failed to progress beyond the fourth round in Paris. At The Championships, however, she had been on her game from the start and followed up her thrilling victory over Kerber with a quarter-final win over an even more experienced opponent, beating Svetlana Kuznetsova 6-3, 6-4. The match was always tight, but Muguruza held firm on her serve and broke Kuznetsova in the fourth game of the first set and the fifth game of the second. In the cool and damp conditions it was more difficult to put away winners, but Muguruza proved that she could play the longer game when required.

Muguruza said that learning how to control her emotions and handle big matches had given her renewed confidence. "It's also a combination of not being too anxious, not being too nervous, trying to free your mind, just trying to concentrate on the tennis part, not about everything else," she said.

Slovakia's Magdalena Rybarikova, the world No.87, kept her incredible run going all the way to the semi-finals with victory over CoCo Vandeweghe on first No.1 Court then Centre Court

Novak Djokovic started proceedings on Centre Court by winning his fourth round encounter with Adrian Mannarino, a match held over from the previous evening

Because of the bad weather the fourth quarter-final was a drawn-out affair. Magdalena Rybarikova and CoCo Vandeweghe started on No. 1 Court but were forced off by rain shortly after 4pm with the score at 2-2 in the second set. With no sign of any improvement in the weather the match was switched under cover to Centre Court, where it resumed more than three hours later.

There was no stopping Rybarikova, however, as the 28-year-old Slovakian won 6-3, 6-3 to continue her remarkable grass court season, which had now brought her 18 wins from 19 matches. Both women showed a willingness to attack the net, but whereas Rybarikova was a model of consistency, Vandeweghe made too many mistakes. Rybarikova said she had been less nervous than when she had played in the previous month's International Tennis Federation tournament at Surbiton.

As the world No. 87 Rybarikova became the lowest ranked player to reach the semi-finals since Zheng Jie, then the world No. 133, in 2008. "I've been dreaming about it since I was a little kid, to be in the semi-finals at Wimbledon," Rybarikova said. "Wimbledon is my favourite Grand Slam, that's for sure. Also playing on grass, it's my favourite surface."

It had been a long day on Centre Court given that Novak Djokovic and Adrian Mannarino had opened proceedings at midday with their fourth round match, which had been held over from the previous day. With rain in the air, it was the first full match of the Fortnight to be played under the roof. Djokovic, who won 6-2, 7-6(5), 6-4, was on top from the moment he broke in the second game of the match, though Mannarino fought back well in the second set. Having recovered an early break of serve, the 29-year-old Frenchman led 4-2 in the tie-break, only to lose five of the next six points.

Djokovic, however, was not in the best of moods despite reaching his ninth Wimbledon quarter-final. The former champion, who called for the doctor after apparently feeling unwell in the first set, thought it had been "the wrong decision" not to move the match to Centre Court the previous evening, said the playing surface was "not in a great condition" and did not want to go into details about an injury for which he had taken a medical time-out in the third set, when a trainer worked on his right shoulder. "It's been something that I've been dragging back and forth for a while now, but I'm still managing to play, which is the most important thing," he said.

Made in Chelsea

CHAMPIONSHIPS
Day 8
NOTEBOOK

Chelsea Pensioners study the Order of Play. Were they trying to discover the best court to have a selfie taken?

• **Johanna Konta's ever-growing popularity** took another lovely upward spike when, after her brilliant triumph over Simona Halep, she made a Chelsea Pensioner's day by having a selfie taken with 72-year-old John Griffiths as she was departing Centre Court.

What really endeared Jo to everyone was the way she helped John by taking the selfie herself when she realised he was struggling with his camera phone. He was a picture of joy when he punched the air after grabbing the shot that went around the world.

• **Novak Djokovic, having belatedly reached the quarter-finals** with his win over Adrian Mannarino, declared himself in favour of fifth set tie-breaks to decide matches.

The old debate reared its head again after Djokovic's fourth round tie was held over on Monday as the Rafael Nadal-Gilles Muller marathon on No.1 Court eventually ran to a 28-game final set.

"Because [John] Isner and [Nicolas] Mahut made history with an 11-hour match once – is that a reason why we're keeping it?" asked the three-time champion.

"It is great drama for a spectator but for a player to play a five, six-hour match, then come back the next day or within two days and perform, it's not really what your body's looking for."

If anyone ever needed a hand it had to be the now legendary Poncho Man

• **On a day when rain left players and spectators feeling frustrated,** a new champion thankfully emerged to help keep everyone entertained. He came in the unlikely shape of an unfortunate gentleman trying every which way to don his rain gear while the heavens opened above No.2 Court during the third round mixed doubles match between Martina Hingis and Jamie Murray and the Czech pair of Roman Jebavy and Lucie Hradecka. All hail Poncho Man!

The spectator's unequal struggle with his waterproof – which saw him battling for 45 seconds somewhere deep within the folds of the garment – prompted much hilarity among the BBC commentary team before he finally gave up his battle and flung aside the poncho in disgust. Soon millions on the internet were enjoying the struggles of one of the Fortnight's favourite characters too.

DAY 9

WEDNESDAY 12 JULY

The names of Andy Murray and Novak Djokovic had become almost permanent fixtures in the Wimbledon story over the last decade. Since 2008 there had not been a gentlemen's singles semi-final line-up that did not include at least one of them and since 2010 either or both of them had appeared in every final.

Previous pages: The Hill was packed full of supporters hoping to cheer Andy Murray to yet another victory at SW19

Above: The world No.1 had been battling through the pain barrier throughout The Championships, and his quarter-final clash with the big-serving American Sam Querrey (**right**) proved a bridge too far

As the Briton and the Serb prepared to face Sam Querrey and Tomas Berdych respectively in the 2017 quarter-finals, few would have imagined that situation was about to change. Murray, the world No.1 and defending champion, had beaten Querrey in seven of their eight previous meetings. Berdych, meanwhile, had lost 25 of his 27 matches against Djokovic, who had won Wimbledon three times in the previous six years.

This, however, was an occasion when the underdogs had their day. Querrey and Berdych secured their places in the last four, while the manner of the exits of Murray and Djokovic raised concerns over their ongoing injury problems. Long recognised as two of the modern game's finest athletes, Murray and Djokovic both left the All England Club clearly in need of rest and recuperation.

Murray, who had been dealing with a hip injury throughout the grass court season, was evidently in physical difficulty by the end of his 6-3, 4-6, 7-6(4), 1-6, 1-6 defeat to Querrey, while Djokovic was forced to retire early in the second set against Berdych after suffering a recurrence of an injury to his right elbow which had been troubling him for the last 18 months.

IT'S OVER TO YOU, JO

As a hobbling Andy Murray bowed out of The Championships, Johanna Konta quickly discovered what it is like to be a home hopeful shouldering the hopes of an entire nation at Wimbledon.

For the first time in 12 years Murray was not to be the last Briton standing in the singles draw, and his defeat by No.24 seed Sam Querrey saw only further pressure heaped on Konta, who spent the day practising at Aorangi Park in preparation for her semi-final against Venus Williams the following afternoon.

The 26-year-old was beginning to sample the madness that Murray has long had to endure during the Fortnight as 'Kontamania' started to truly take hold. Everything, from the fascination with her home-baked muffins to her support from rock stars on social media, left her feeling "very excited and very humbled".

And amid his disappointment, Murray could still spare a thought for Konta's great challenge. "I hope she goes on to win the tournament," he said after his loss. "She's certainly got a fantastic chance. I saw quite a lot of her match yesterday [against Simona Halep] – she played extremely well under a lot of pressure and if she keeps playing like that there's no reason why she can't do it."

Johanna Konta (above) practises in preparation for her semi-final with Venus Williams in the knowledge that the whole nation will be behind her

Although Murray had been walking with a limp since before the start of The Championships, he had been moving well enough in matches and was through to the quarter-finals for the 10th year in a row. However, he had not been taken to five sets and had not faced as consistent a big hitter as Querrey.

When Murray won the first seven points, took the opening set in 28 minutes and went a break up in the second there was little sign of the difficulties ahead. Even after Querrey had fought back to take the second set Murray went on to win the third. However, from 1-1 in the fourth Murray's hip injury took its toll. The Scot was unable to generate his usual power off his groundstrokes, his serve speed dropped and he could not move with his usual fluency. Querrey, serving with great power and going for his shots, won 21 out of 24 points at one stage and 11 of the last 12 games.

Following his victory over Djokovic in the third round 12 months earlier, the 29-year-old had now beaten the world No.1 and defending champion two years in a row. The world No.28 was through to his first semi-final in his 42nd Grand Slam tournament, a record for the Open era, and was the first American man to reach a singles semi-final at one of the four majors since Andy Roddick at Wimbledon in 2009. "It's a really big deal," Querrey said. "It's my first [Grand Slam] semi-final. To beat Andy, to have it be at Wimbledon, was even a little more special. It was just an incredible match."

Murray, who had never previously lost at The Championships to an opponent ranked outside the world's top 19, paid credit to the 6ft 6in American, saying how well he had served at the end. The Scot said he had been advised that he would not cause any serious damage to his hip by playing and was proud that he had given his all. "The whole tournament I've been a little bit sore, but I tried my best right to the end," he said. "I almost found a way to get into the semis."

Above: Novak Djokovic cut a forlorn figure as his chronic elbow problem flared up and forced him to retire when a set and a break down to Tomas Berdych

Below: After a difficult season, Berdych – the 2010 finalist – was exultant at reaching the Wimbledon semi-finals for the second year in succession

Without going into details about the injury, Murray said it had been a long-term problem. "As you get older, things are a little bit tougher to manage than they are when you're younger," he said. "There's a bit more wear and tear there. I've managed to deal with it for a very long time. I'm sure moving forward I'll be able to get through it. I just need to do all of the right things and be even more diligent and professional than I have been recently."

Djokovic, who retired when trailing Berdych 6-7(2), 0-2, had spent more than two hours on the treatment table before the match. He revealed afterwards that his elbow had been troubling him again since the very start of the tournament. He said the pain had been getting worse and affected his serve and forehand in particular.

"I'm just going to talk with specialists, as I have done in the last year or so, try to figure out what's the best way to treat it and to solve it, to find a long-term solution," Djokovic said. He said he would consider taking a break but added: "The specialists that I've talked with, they haven't been really too clear, mentioning also surgery, mentioning different options."

Berdych had lost his previous 19 matches against top five opponents. The 31-year-old Czech, who had dropped to No.15 in the world rankings after a previous unbroken run of six years in the top 10, said his place in the semi-finals was a reward for all his hard work. He reached his only Grand Slam final at The Championships 2010, losing in straight sets to Rafael Nadal, having beaten Roger Federer in the quarter-finals and Djokovic in the semi-finals.

Roger Federer's semi-final defeat by Milos Raonic in last year's gentlemen's singles signalled the end of his 2016 season, but rejuvenated after a period of rest the Swiss master put his Canadian opponent to the sword in 2017

His semi-final opponent this time would be Federer, who met Milos Raonic at The Championships for the third time in four years. Federer's 6-4, 6-2, 7-6(4) victory came in his 100th match at the All England Club, a gentlemen's singles total bettered in the Open era only by Jimmy Connors' 102. Raonic, the runner-up in 2016, had five break points but could not convert any of them. He was also unable to capitalise on a 3-0 lead in the tie-break at the end of the third set as Federer turned on the style with some stunning shots, including a forehand winner down the line which he bent like a David Beckham free kick.

Federer expressed sympathy for Murray and Djokovic and stressed how much he had benefited from the six months he had taken off at the end of 2016. "I'm playing very well, I'm rested, I'm fresh, I'm confident too," Federer said. "I'm much better prepared for Wimbledon this year than last year. Last year I had a hard, hard time practising through the clay court season. The grass court season was difficult because of the back issues I had, and the knee issues. I was lacking practice really. Then in the matches I could never really play quite so freely because I was more focused on how the knee was behaving than on how I needed to hit my forehand or backhand, or what was not going to be good for my opponent. This year I'm just a normal tennis player again where I can focus on tactics."

While Federer was through to his 12th gentlemen's singles semi-final – an Open era record, beating Connors' mark of 11 – Marin Cilic, appearing in The Championships for the 11th time, reached his first semi-final by beating Gilles Muller 3-6, 7-6(6), 7-5, 5-7, 6-1. In the Open era only Jonas Bjorkman, Cilic's coach, made more appearances (13) before reaching his first semi-final.

Milos Raonic strained every sinew against Federer but ended up sighing after a comprehensive defeat: "I did everything I could, I tried... he's doing a lot of things well"

Marin Cilic roared his delight
after negotiating a bruising
five-setter on No.1 Court
against Rafael Nadal's
conqueror, Gilles Muller

Muller went into his quarter-final knowing he had won more tour-level grass court singles matches (11) in the current season than any other man. However, he might also have been aware of the fact that the last six players to beat Nadal before the final at The Championships had lost in the next round. Following his five-set victory over the Spaniard in the fourth round, the world No.26 became embroiled in another marathon against Cilic. In a high-octane contest between two big servers there were only four breaks of serve in the first four sets, but Cilic's durability proved crucial as the Croatian won the first five games of the decider.

Cilic said that he had been more confident ever since he won his first Grand Slam title at Flushing Meadows in 2014. "Preparation-wise I believe in my own abilities," he said. "I believe when coming to these stages of the tournament, I'm going to still be able to play great tennis. I know I have it in me that I can win. That's extremely important. For the other part I think it's also extremely important to be mentally fresh, mentally ready. It's a matter of a few points here and there that can make a huge difference. In these last couple of months I believe I've been really mentally focused every single match, which has helped me to get to the point where I'm little bit stronger mentally. I believe that can make a huge difference."

In doubles it was a day for Henri Kontinen, the world No.1, to stamp his authority. In the gentlemen's doubles the Finn and his partner, John Peers, moved into the semi-finals with a hard-fought 6-4, 6-7(5), 6-7(4), 7-6(7), 6-1 win over Ryan Harrison and Michael Venus. In the mixed event Kontinen and Heather Watson, the defending champions, reached the quarter-finals by beating the No.4 seeds, Ivan Dodig and Sania Mirza, 7-6(4), 6-4. The British wild cards Ken Skupski and Jocelyn Rae beat the No.12 seeds, Max Mirnyi and Ekaterina Makarova, 5-7, 6-4, 9-7 to earn a meeting with the No.1 seeds, Jamie Murray and Martina Hingis.

The class of '67

Rod Laver was among the pioneers from the 1967 'Wimbledon Pro' tournament, which paved the way for the Open era, who were invited to the Royal Box by AELTC Chairman Philip Brook

● **Half a century on from a tournament** that changed the face of tennis, the trailblazers of 1967 returned to Wimbledon to take their places in the Royal Box as special guests of the Chairman. Butch Buchholz, Andres Gimeno, Dennis Ralston, Rod Laver, Ken Rosewall, Fred Stolle, Jenny Hoad, the widow of Lew Hoad, and Rita Agassi, widow of Pancho Gonzales, watched the action on Centre Court and reflected on the 'Wimbledon Pro' event held in August 1967 that paved the way for the first Open Championships the following year.

Back then many of the sport's biggest names were ineligible for Wimbledon and the other Grand Slams because they had turned professional, but Herman David – the forward-thinking chairman of the All England Club – drove the idea of staging the 'Wimbledon World Lawn Professional Championships', which brought eight top men's players together in a hugely successful televised event that drew 30,000 through the gates and saw Laver beat Rosewall in a classic final that helped usher in a new era for the sport. "That started the ball rolling – and Wimbledon made it happen," the great Laver happily recalled.

● **It was a big day for Luxembourg** as Gilles Muller did battle with Marin Cilic for a historic semi-final place. Citizens of the Grand Duchy flocked to screenings of the match on big screens in the capital Luxembourg City and near Muller's home town of Leudelange, while Prince Guillaume and Prime Minister Xavier Bettel were in the

No.1 Court stands cheering on the 34-year-old known to all Luxembourgers as 'Mulles'. Alas for an expectant nation, Cilic was to end the fairytale.

● **How do wizards learn their trade?** They go and observe another wizard working his magic, that's how. So it was then that watching Roger Federer in action against Milos Raonic from the Royal Box were Gandalf, also known as Sir Ian

Gandalf – aka Sir Ian McKellen – had his eyes trained on another wizard on Centre Court

McKellen, and Professor McGonagall, in the shape of Dame Maggie Smith. Acting royalty, by any standards...

● **Andy Murray's stock around the game rose** even further despite the loss of his Wimbledon crown after he corrected a journalist who had carelessly suggested that his conqueror Sam Querrey had just become the first American to reach a major semi-final since 2009.

"Male player," interrupted Murray, to the delight of those who felt it was a little rich to forget – for instance – how Serena Williams alone had won 14 Grand Slam titles in the last eight years.

Serena herself led the tributes to the Scot in effusive fashion: "I do not think there is a woman player who is not totally supportive of Andy Murray. He has spoken up for women's issues and women's rights, especially in tennis, forever. He has done it again. We love Andy Murray."

"That's my boy," Judy Murray tweeted.

DAY
10
THURSDAY
13 JULY

T

The company had been welcome while it lasted, but now Johanna Konta was on her own. After Andy Murray's quarter-final defeat to Sam Querrey the previous day, Konta, for the first time in her life, was the last British player left in singles competition at The Championships.

Previous pages: Centre Court watches with baited breath as Johanna Konta takes on five-time Ladies' Singles champion Venus Williams

Above: Konta gave it everything but her bid to become the first Briton to make the Ladies' Singles Final for 40 years finally foundered against the 37-year-old American icon

Newspapers probably never find their way into the famous 'bubble' that Konta inhabits during tournaments, but if they had done so even her ability to cope with pressure might have been tested. Two headlines in the *Daily Express* summed it up. One described her as "the new darling of Centre Court" and another read: "Fallen Andy calls on Jo to claim crown".

Having become the first Briton to reach the quarter-finals of the ladies' singles since Jo Durie in 1984 and then the first to make the semi-finals since Virginia Wade in 1978, Konta had one more hurdle to clear if she was to become the first to play in the final since Wade's triumph in 1977. On the other side of the net, however, was one of the game's legends and a player who was still making history at the age of 37. Having won the last of her five Wimbledon singles titles in 2008, Venus Williams was attempting to become the oldest finalist in the ladies' singles for 23 years.

Konta and Williams had met five times in the previous two years. The American had won in Wuhan in 2015 and in Rome in their most recent encounter, but Konta had won in the Australian Open first round in 2016, when she went on to reach the semi-finals, in the 2016 final at Stanford and in the semi-finals of the 2017 Miami Open on her way to the biggest title of her career to date.

The odds appeared to favour the Briton, but to the disappointment of most in the Centre Court crowd, some of whom were wearing 'Konta Mania' t-shirts, Williams took control from the start. Twenty years after making her debut at The Championships, Williams dictated the points with her relentless power and accuracy from the back of the court, in defiance of those who had believed that she could win only by attacking the net. The world No.11 made only nine unforced errors. Konta, unable to find any rhythm, struggled to cope with Williams' damaging body serves and found herself under regular attack on her own second serve. Williams won 6-4, 6-2 in just 73 minutes.

Konta briefly threatened at 4-4 in the first set, but Williams saved the second of the Briton's only break points of the match with a 106mph second serve, which was the fastest second serve either woman hit all afternoon. Taking advantage of some costly errors, Williams broke in the following game to take the first set. Konta rarely looked like getting back into the match as Williams broke again in the fourth and eighth games of the second set to secure her victory.

Venus Williams moved just a win away from becoming the oldest Ladies' Singles champion for 109 years

"She dictated the match from the very first ball till the very last one," Konta said afterwards. "I think she just showed her true qualities and why she's a five-time champion here, just a true champion that she is. It was very difficult for me to get a good foothold in the match. The few opportunities that I did get, she did incredibly well to take them away from me. I don't think I did too much wrong out there. I think it was all credit to her." The Briton was pleased with her work over the Fortnight. "I definitely feel like there's no reason why I would not be able to be in a position to win a title like this one day," she said.

For Williams, meanwhile, this was another extraordinary chapter in her extraordinary story, which had appeared to be drawing to a sorry ending six years previously when she announced that she had been diagnosed with Sjögren's syndrome, an incurable auto-immune condition that causes fatigue and joint pain. In order to manage the condition Williams had to adapt her training and her diet. "I had a lot of issues," she admitted. "There have definitely been a lot of ups and downs. I just try to hold my head up high, no matter what is happening in life." She added: "In sport especially, you have injuries. You have illnesses. You're not going to be always playing 100 per cent. If I decide to walk out on the court, I try to just compete that day."

Even after dropping out of the world's top 100 in 2011, Williams continued to believe that she could compete at the highest level. At The Championships 2016 she reached her first Grand Slam semi-final for seven years and at this year's Australian Open she played in her first Grand Slam singles final for eight years before losing to her sister, Serena. Now she had reached her first Wimbledon singles final since 2009, when she had again lost to Serena. "This year has been amazing in terms of my play, playing deep into the big events," she said. "Of course, I'm excited about being in another final again. I'll try to take it a step further."

Williams' opponent in the final would be Garbiñe Muguruza, who needed just 64 minutes to crush Magdalena Rybarikova 6-1, 6-1. Muguruza, who won 60 points to Rybarikova's 33, was aggressive throughout. Most of the rallies were short and sweet as the 23-year-old Spaniard pushed her opponent back with big groundstrokes, her backhand down the line proving particularly effective. With Muguruza attacking the net and Rybarikova looking nervous, the 2015 runner-up went 3-0 up in just 10 minutes and led 5-0 before her opponent finally won a game. The second set followed a similar pattern as Muguruza raced into a 4-0 lead before closing out victory on her second match point. "I stepped on the court super-confident and I played well," she said afterwards.

For the first time in the tournament Rybarikova had looked like the player who had made seven consecutive first round exits from The Championships between 2008 and 2014 rather than the one who had won 18 of her first 19 matches of the 2017 grass court season. "It was a very difficult match for me," the Slovakian said afterwards. "Garbiñe played an amazing match. I've never seen her play that well."

It was hard to believe that Muguruza had arrived at The Championships having lost 1-6, 0-6 to Barbora Strycova in the first round at Eastbourne in the previous week, but the Spaniard demonstrated the ability to put disappointments behind her. She had done the same after the previous month's French Open, where her defence of the title had ended in a fourth round defeat to Kristina Mladenovic. "Once that tournament was over, I just changed the page," Muguruza said. "It was a different situation for me going into a Grand Slam as a defending champion. It was just a good experience. No matter how it ended up, it was good to have that behind me and to look forward again for new objectives. It was something big to deal with."

Opposite: The moment it dawned on Venus Williams that she had reached a ninth Wimbledon Ladies' Singles Final, eight years since her last and an incredible 17 years since her first

Below: Magdalena Rybarikova was woken rudely from her dream-like Wimbledon by Garbiñe Muguruza, who allowed her just two games in their semi-final

Garbiñe Muguruza powered her way to her second Ladies' Singles Final in three years, raising the prospect that she could go on to emulate her coaching adviser, Conchita Martinez, who in 1994 became the first Spanish woman to lift the Venus Rosewater Dish

American tennis stars Alice Marble (right) and Katharine Winthrop were agog at seeing a BBC camera installed on Centre Court for the first time in 1937

A SPECIAL RELATIONSHIP

Ninety years since the first radio broadcast, 80 years after the first TV transmission and 50 years from the first screening in colour, The Championships 2017 was unquestionably the time to celebrate the long and fruitful partnership between the BBC and Wimbledon.

The longest-running sports rights agreement in the world saw the BBC showing more live coverage than ever before at this edition of The Championships, with Sue Barker – a ladies' singles semi-finalist here in 1977 now in her 24th year at the BBC – leading the TV coverage, while BBC Radio 5 live broadcast 100 hours of action and the BBC Sport website and app hosted 15 live HD video streams across the Fortnight.

The trio of anniversaries were celebrated in an exhibition at the Wimbledon Lawn Tennis Museum, where visitors could follow the evolution of the partnership from the earliest days of the radio 'running commentary' of Captain Henry Blythe Thornhill 'Teddy' Wakelam. Ten years after Wakelam's first pioneering broadcast, 2,000 viewers got their first glimpse of tennis on TV as British star Bunny Austin took on George Lyttleton-Rogers on Centre Court.

By 1967, colour TV was all the rage. As the great broadcaster Sir David Attenborough – who led the revolution as the then BBC Two Controller – explained at the exhibition launch, the reason Europe's first colour transmission came from SW19 was because, short of colour cameras, it dawned on the BBC that with just three they could shoot "hours and hours"

of Centre Court drama: "Because of Wimbledon, and those three cameras, we beat everyone to the punch. So from the BBC's point of view: Wimbledon, we love you, and we thank you!"

The feeling remains mutual, with the good news being that, after agreeing an extension to their partnership, the special relationship will continue to at least 2024.

Tony Hall, Director-General of the BBC, presents AELTC Chief Executive Richard Lewis (left) with a special BBC Sports Personality camera trophy to mark the partnership between the two institutions

Muguruza's regular coach, Sam Sumyk, did not travel to The Championships because he wanted to be with his wife, who was about to give birth. Instead it was Muguruza's Fed Cup captain, Conchita Martinez, the 1994 Wimbledon champion, who took charge of her coaching and passed on lessons from her own experiences. "She's helping me to deal with the stress of the tournament, because it's a long tournament," Muguruza said. "She just knows how to prepare, how to train, what to do. To have her by my side, someone who has won before, also gives me this little bit of confidence."

Muguruza said that she talked to Sumyk every day. "Conchita and Sam are really working together," she said. "They are in contact. Before I do something, they both decide on it. I think I'm here because I've been working not only the last few days, but for a longer time, getting ready for this kind of moment."

Lukasz Kubot and Marcelo Melo extended their unbeaten run on grass to reach the final of the gentlemen's doubles. The Brazilian and the Pole, who won the titles at 's-Hertogenbosch and Halle, beat the No.1 seeds, Henri Kontinen and John Peers, 6-3, 6-7(4), 6-2, 4-6, 9-7 to set up a final showdown with Austria's Oliver Marach and Croatia's Mate Pavic, who beat Nikola Mektic and Franko Skugor 4-6, 7-5, 7-6(4), 3-6, 17-15 after more than four-and-a-half hours.

Kontinen teamed up later in the day with Heather Watson to continue the defence of their mixed doubles title. The Finn and the Briton edged a tight encounter with Rohan Bopanna and Gabriela Dabrowski, winning 6-7(4), 6-4, 7-5 to set up a semi-final meeting with Bruno Soares and Elena Vesnina. Jamie Murray and Martina Hingis proved too strong for Ken Skupski and Jocelyn Rae, winning 6-4, 6-4 to secure a semi-final against Marcelo Demoliner and Maria Jose Martinez Sanchez.

As the Gentlemen's Wheelchair Singles got under way Sweden's Stefan Olsson avenged his defeat by Gordon Reid in the 2016 final, beating the No.1 seed 6-2, 6-3. Argentina's Gustavo Fernandez, playing his first match since becoming world No.1, beat Stephane Houdet 6-2, 6-4. The No.1 seed in the Ladies' Wheelchair Singles also went out as Aniek van Koot beat her fellow Dutchwoman, Jiske Griffioen, 6-3, 6-2. Yui Kamiji, the No.2 seed, beat Lucy Shuker 6-3, 6-1.

Scotland's No.1 seed Gordon Reid saw his reign as Gentlemen's Wheelchair Singles champion ended by the man he beat in the 2016 final, Sweden's Stefan Olsson

Martina's still got it

The 60-year-old heart is still willing – even if the body sometimes lets the great Martina Navratilova down

● **The way Martina Navratilova dived** across the turf during her Ladies' Invitation Doubles match it was as if we were being transported back in time to when she was Wimbledon's undisputed queen of the serve and volley.

However, the lady in question didn't quite see it that way...

"My strength is that I have no weaknesses," the great nine-time Ladies' Singles champion – who first competed at The Championships 44 years ago – joked, "other than I'm very slow, I can't jump as high and my serve can't crack an egg!"

Ah, but you could still see the competitive juices swilling around during her outing alongside Cara Black against Andrea Jaeger and Conchita Martinez. "I'm still playing the way I used to. I just don't hit it as hard or move as well," Navratilova said. "But it's fun!" Judging by the smiling faces around the No.1 Court crowd, the SW19 faithful agreed.

● **Johanna Konta's wonderful breakthrough** at Wimbledon might have been ended by Venus Williams, but Eastbourne's finest was able to find some solace in music.

Her coach Wim Fissette told The Wimbledon Channel how exciting life has become for Konta as she'd received an invitation from her beloved U2 to go backstage at one of their concerts, while she had also had her picture taken with singer Ellie Goulding and been tweeted by no less a tennis-loving rock god than Mick Jagger.

And after the loss to Venus, the mighty Van Morrison also took to Twitter after learning that the green-eyed girl – not brown-eyed, sadly – was a fan of his and invited Konta to one of his concerts "as my guest". Naturally, she accepted instantly.

"Jo said to me, 'Suddenly I'm getting so many friends!'" laughed an impressed Fissette.

● **"Tough day at the office today for me,"** Magdalena Rybarikova posted on Instagram after her stellar run to the semi-finals was ended ruthlessly by Garbiñe Muguruza.

Still, though, there was a happy ending to her Cinderella story. As she was waiting at the competitors' transport desk to leave, Roger Federer popped by and posed for a photo. "Made my day a little easier," Rybarikova observed. Goodness, a Good Samaritan too? Can the man do no wrong?

A photo with Roger Federer can make it a better day for anyone

● **Having ended the hopes** of one Briton in Johanna Konta, Venus Williams now had another in her sights. Back in 1908, Ealing's Charlotte Cooper Sterry won the last of her five Wimbledon ladies' singles titles at the age of 37, the last four of those won after she had developed severe hearing difficulties. Now Williams – like Cooper, a 37-year-old five-time champion, an Olympic gold medallist and a tremendous fighter who had overcome worrying health problems – was one match away from becoming the oldest winner since 'Chattie' 109 years earlier.

DAY
11

FRIDAY
14 JULY

The semi-final line-up for the gentlemen's singles featured four familiar faces, but in one respect it suggested that we were living in changing times. For the first time since 2003 none of the semi-finalists at a Grand Slam tournament were ranked in the world's top four.

Previous pages: The feeling when you've just reached a Wimbledon final. Marin Cilic savoured the greatest moment of his career since winning the 2014 US Open after defeating Sam Querrey in the semi-final

Roger Federer was the No.3 seed, but only by dint of his grass court form over the last two years. The 35-year-old Swiss was No.5 in the world rankings, 10 places ahead of his opponent, Tomas Berdych. In the other semi-final Marin Cilic, the world No.6, would take on Sam Querrey, the world No.28.

While Federer's position was clearly not a reflection of his recent form – he was no higher than No.5 because he had not earned any ranking points in the second half of 2016 during his six-month break – the absence from the semi-finals of Andy Murray, Rafael Nadal, Stan Wawrinka and Novak Djokovic told its own story. Three of the world's top four were nursing injuries, which was perhaps a sign of their advancing years, while the fourth, Nadal, had struggled on grass because of his troublesome knees ever since his last appearance in the final in 2011. For the first time ever the top four men in the singles rankings were all over the age of 30.

Taking 35-year-old Federer out of the equation, the three other semi-finalists were not representatives of a younger generation sweeping aside the old guard but contemporaries of the so-called 'Big Four' (or 'Big Five' if you included Wawrinka). For years they had lived off the scraps left behind by their illustrious rivals. The domination of the Big Four was particularly evident at The Championships, where they had won the title every year since 2002.

Berdych, aged 31, had played in 54 Grand Slam tournaments and reached just one final, losing to Nadal at Wimbledon in 2010. Cilic had won the 2014 US Open, but in his 37 other Grand Slam appearances the 28-year-old Croat had never gone beyond the quarter-finals. Querrey, aged 29, was through to his first semi-final in his 42nd Grand Slam tournament, a record for the Open era.

Federer, who had been in some of the best form of his life since returning to competition in Australia in January, tried – not very convincingly – to play down his status as the favourite for the title. "These other guys are all big hitters," he said in assessing the semi-final line-up. "They've got big serves, big forehands, big hitters really. All three guys are taller and stronger than I am."

Berdych had played Federer 24 times previously. He had beaten the Swiss twice at Grand Slam level, at Wimbledon in 2010 and the US Open in 2012, but lost their last seven meetings. It was therefore no surprise when Federer extended that winning run, though Berdych could take consolation from the fact that he gave the seven-time champion his toughest challenge of The Championships 2017 to date. Federer, roared on by the vast majority of a passionate Centre Court crowd, won 7-6(4), 7-6(4), 6-4, but had to survive some difficult moments, particularly when Berdych got the better of many of their baseline exchanges.

Left: Tomas Berdych had said he would be up against the "greatest of them all" in Roger Federer, and his description proved accurate as Federer turned on the style to claim victory in straight sets

Below: Federer reached a record 11th Gentlemen's Singles Final at Wimbledon and his 29th Grand Slam final in all with his victory over Berdych

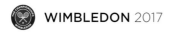
Berdych retrieved an early break of serve in the opening set and was pushing hard in the first tie-break until a bad forehand miss put Federer 5-3 ahead. The Swiss took a grip on the second tie-break when three successive forehand winners took him into a 4-1 lead. At 2-3 and 15-40 down in the third set Federer hit aces on three of the next four points to dig himself out of trouble and then broke in the following game to put himself on the road to victory.

"This guy doesn't really seem to be getting any older or slowing down at all," Berdych said afterwards. "I think I played really good tennis throughout the whole tournament, but unfortunately I faced a guy who was playing his best. I think he's playing by far the best tennis right now."

Roger Federer salutes the crowd after moving to within one match of lifting a record eighth gentlemen's singles title but still had plenty of time to sign a few autographs before leaving Centre Court

At 35 years and 342 days Federer would become the second oldest man in the Open era to play in the Wimbledon singles final after Ken Rosewall, who lost to Jimmy Connors in 1974 aged 39 years and 246 days. He also extended two of his own records by reaching his 11th Wimbledon final and his 29th final in all Grand Slam tournaments. Now he would have the chance to become the first man in history to win the All England Club's gentlemen's singles title eight times.

"It makes me really happy, making history here at Wimbledon." Federer said after his victory. "It's a big deal. I love this tournament. All my dreams came true here as a player. To have another chance to go for number eight now, to be so close now at this stage, is a great feeling. I'm unbelievably excited. I hope I can play one more good match. Eleven finals here, all these records, it's great. But it doesn't give me the title quite yet. That's why I came here this year. I'm so close now. I've just got to stay focused."

You've got to laugh

Amid all the deadly serious stuff during the business end of The Championships, it's always a huge delight to wander around the Grounds and take in the Invitation events.

What's better then seeing some great names, including seven Gentlemen's and Ladies' Singles champions in Martina Navratilova, Conchita Martinez, Marion Bartoli, Lindsay Davenport, Goran Ivanisevic, Richard Krajicek and Lleyton Hewitt, strutting their stuff on court once again while letting their hair down a bit?

And although some of their antics, as evidenced here, suggest the match results perhaps weren't taken too seriously, the watching spectators definitely noticed that the competitive fires were still burning brightly at times. Why else do you think Navratilova, Hewitt and Krajicek – players who have always hated losing a point, let alone a match – all qualified for Sunday's finals?

Top: Wayne Ferreira and Goran Ivanisevic and their opponents Jeremy Bates and Chris Wilkinson all seemingly required a lie-down during their match on No.3 Court

Middle: Kim Clijsters and Rennae Stubbs seemed to be having a rare old laugh during their match against Cara Black and Martina Navratilova

Right: Michael Llodra felt he needed an armchair ride while serving alongside Mansour Bahrami

Above: Sam Querrey powered down a total of 13 aces and 46 winners against Marin Cilic

Opposite, top: No man in the Open era had played in more Championships before reaching his first singles final than the 28-year-old Croat

Opposite, bottom: Querrey and Cilic shook hands after what was for them a relatively short battle as Cilic prevailed in two hours and 56 minutes – a sprint compared to when he won in five-and-a-half hours in 2012

His opponent in the final would be Cilic, who beat Querrey 6-7(6), 6-4, 7-6(3), 7-5 in a heavyweight contest full of thunderous serves and booming groundstrokes. Querrey's fastest serve was timed at 135mph and Cilic's at 134mph. However, after an opening set in which there had been no break points Cilic started to get the measure of Querrey's serve. The world No.6 also found a good rhythm from the baseline and hit 70 winners to the American's 46.

Cilic made the first break of serve in the seventh game of the second set and won the tie-break at the end of the third set after Querrey made two successive unforced errors when he served at 3-4. After an early exchange of breaks in the fourth set Querrey went 15-40 down at 5-6 after a double fault and two more unforced errors. Cilic hit a forehand winner on his second match point to secure victory after nearly three hours.

If Cilic had looked closely at his draw at the start of the tournament he would have seen that the seedings suggested he would need to beat Kei Nishikori, Nadal and Murray if he was to reach the final. However, the draw opened up beautifully for the Croat, whose highest ranked opponent en route to the final was Roberto Bautista Agut, the world No.19. It is always true, nevertheless, that you can only beat the opponents you face and Cilic demonstrated admirable self-belief after losing in the quarter-finals in each of the three previous years.

Cilic, whose coach, Jonas Bjorkman, suffered semi-final disappointment at The Championships with Murray in 2015, thought his mental toughness had been crucial to his success over the Fortnight. He added:

"My tennis in the last several weeks is really on a high level and that has given me a lot of consistency with my mindset."

He also felt he had been learning from his defeats. "It's tough when you're losing, but the losses are giving you a clearer picture compared with when you are winning," Cilic said. "When you are winning, everything is great. You don't look too much on the bad stuff. But over the course of my career, especially in the last few years, I felt that I matured a little bit more in dealing with losses, especially on the big stages, in the big tournaments. I feel that just taking small details out of those matches has helped me to become better. Obviously I use that in situations when I come to [face players] again."

The world No.6 said it would mean the world to him to win Wimbledon. "When I won the US Open in 2014, it just opened up so many possibilities in my mind for the rest of my career," he said. "To be able to do it again would definitely mean even more because I know how much it meant for me to win that first one. It would be absolutely a dream come true to win Wimbledon."

Britain's Alfie Hewett celebrates after he and Gordon Reid defeated Argentina's Gustavo Fernandez and Japan's Shingo Kunieda in the Gentlemen's Wheelchair Doubles (**above**), while Japan's Yui Kamiji lost to Germany's Sabine Ellerbrock in the Ladies' Wheelchair Singles (**right**)

Although Andy Murray and Johanna Konta had not made it to the famed Finals weekend, Britain would have two finalists – on opposite sides of the net – in the mixed doubles. Jamie Murray and Switzerland's Martina Hingis were living up to their billing as the No.1 seeds, while Heather Watson and Finland's Henri Kontinen, who were unseeded, were defending their title like tigers. Murray and Hingis eased to a 6-2, 7-5 semi-final victory over Marcelo Demoliner and Maria Jose Martinez Sanchez on Centre Court, while Kontinen and Watson were pushed all the way on No.1 Court before beating Bruno Soares and Elena Vesnina 6-4, 6-7(6), 6-3.

Vesnina won her other semi-final when she partnered Ekaterina Makarova to a 7-5, 6-2 victory over Anna-Lena Groenefeld and Kveta Peschke in the ladies' doubles. Their opponents in the final would be Chan Hao-Ching and Monica Niculescu, who beat Makoto Ninomiya and Renata Voracova 7-6(4), 4-6, 9-7 after nearly three hours.

Argentina's Gustavo Fernandez reached the Gentlemen's Wheelchair Singles Final when he beat Britain's Alfie Hewett 4-6, 7-6(4), 6-3, reversing the result of the final at the previous month's French Open. Sweden's Stefan Olsson won the other semi-final, beating Japan's Shingo Kunieda 6-4, 6-2. Meanwhile, Germany's Sabine Ellerbrock and the Netherlands' Diede de Groot booked their places in the Ladies' Wheelchair Singles Final. Ellerbrock beat Yui Kamiji 7-6(4), 1-6, 7-6(4), while de Groot beat Aniek van Koot 6-0, 6-2.

Dressed to impress

Chris Quinn, Ireland's newest Wimbledon star, took a bow with his accomplices after one of SW19's great spectator interactions

Day 11

● **It normally takes years of work to earn Wimbledon immortality,** but a 46-year-old Irishman named Chris Quinn needed less than five priceless minutes to achieve it after his part in one of the funniest spectacles to ever grace a Championship court.

It all started when four-time Grand Slam champion Kim Clijsters, partnering Rennae Stubbs in the Ladies' Invitation Doubles, was wondering aloud where to serve against Conchita Martinez and Andrea Jaeger only for the spectating Quinn to call out cheekily that she should go with a body serve.

Clijsters had a better idea and suggested the big man come and face a body serve himself. However, after she'd ushered him on she realised his green shirt and blue shorts wouldn't observe the White Clothing and Equipment Rule so she quickly loaned him her spare skirt and top. There followed the wonderful scene of Quinn struggling to squeeze the skirt over his frame as Clijsters and co. fell about helpless with mirth.

The cheerful interloper then proceeded to successfully return the Belgian legend's serve and even replayed the point before the four players all posed for a photo with the new SW19 sensation.

Thanking his new comedy partner Clijsters on Twitter later, Quinn exulted: "I got to play in Wimbledon. One off the bucket list!!" He later auctioned off the prized skirt and top for charity.

● **Sachin Tendulkar knows the feeling of being adored** by a billion people as India's greatest cricketing idol. So he surely has a better understanding than anyone about how his friend Roger Federer handles the mass adulation that swirls around him.

Before watching from the Royal Box as Federer reached yet another final, Tendulkar told The Wimbledon Channel: "As a sportsman and tennis player he is someone the whole world admires but I admire him more as a person. I think he's such a down-to-earth, humble man. After having achieved so much in life, to be like that it's always nice to be around him."

Cricket legend Sachin Tendulkar chatted with England rugby coach Eddie Jones in the Royal Box while watching Roger Federer in action

● **Tomas Berdych was interrogated** at length about what made Federer so great after his semi-final defeat. Did he have any weaknesses, the Czech was asked. "Challenges (to Hawk-Eye)" was all he could come up with.

● **What is it about Formula One world champions** and sartorial troubles at Wimbledon? In 2015 Lewis Hamilton couldn't get into the Royal Box because he wasn't wearing a jacket and tie. This time, reigning champ Nico Rosberg was telling The Wimbledon Channel about his excitement at being invited to the Royal Box when it was pointed out to him he wasn't wearing any socks. "No way! I made such an effort to be dressed adequately," he chuckled, before being given a suitable pair. As it happened, Federer knocked his socks off later anyway...

Anyone who's anyone

It was Hollywood star Hugh Jackman who, after arriving at the All England Club for the first time a few years back, posted a picture on social media with the message: "At Wimbledon. Bucket list – check!!!"

Like the rest of us, it seems, celebrities simply cannot resist the lure of the place. It's a must-visit venue, an arena to see and one where it's almost as good to be seen.

Throughout the Fortnight, The Championships 2017 was proud to welcome royal dignitaries, A-list stars of film and stage or sporting luminaries drinking in the atmosphere that makes Wimbledon so special.

Olly Murs was more than happy to oblige his fans in the London constabulary with a snap (**above**), but as for the green-jacketed Sergio Garcia and David Beckham (**right**), who knows which one of them was after the selfie?

Famous faces flock to The Championships (clockwise from top left): Adventurer Bear Grylls and singer Katherine Jenkins; Sir Cliff Richard; Bee Gees star Barry Gibb; Actress Joely Richardson; Formula One world champion Nico Rosberg; Comedian and author Stephen Fry

DAY
12

SATURDAY
15 JULY

If Garbiñe Muguruza versus Venus Williams was a Ladies' Singles Final that few would have predicted, it was, on reflection, a perfect way to end what had been an enthralling competition. Muguruza, who had proved her grass court credentials by finishing runner-up two years earlier, was one of the most exciting players among a younger generation hoping to take advantage of the absence of two of the biggest names in the women's game, Serena Williams and Maria Sharapova.

Meanwhile Venus Williams, at 37 years and 28 days, was proving that age need not be a barrier to glory. Five times a Wimbledon Ladies' Singles champion, the American was attempting to become the oldest since Charlotte Cooper Sterry in 1908.

The first 11 days of The Championships had been played under largely sunny skies, but rain meant that this would be the first Ladies' Singles Final to be played under the Centre Court's retractable roof. The sound of racket on ball is amplified with the roof in place and with two of the game's hardest hitters trading blows it was almost as if firecrackers were exploding every few seconds.

It was a final of two halves. For the first 10 games there was little to choose between the two players, but the last eight were one-sided as Muguruza won 7-5, 6-0 in just 77 minutes to claim her first Wimbledon title. Williams, who hit an ace on the first point, had the slight edge in the early stages as Muguruza opened her first service game with a double fault and struggled initially to find her range on her forehand. However, the match quickly developed into a big-hitting battle between two outstanding players.

Williams scorned a break point opportunity with a missed forehand in the sixth game, but ultimately the match turned when Muguruza saved two set points at 4-5 and 15-40, the first after a long baseline rally and the second with a service winner. At 5-5 Muguruza made the first break of serve, forcing Williams into errors with some big groundstrokes, and at 6-5 and 30-15 the 23-year-old Spaniard hit the shot of the match when a wonderful backhand lob landed on the baseline. Williams saved the first set point with a powerful forehand but on the second she netted a backhand. Boris Becker said on Twitter that it was one of the best first sets he had seen at Wimbledon. Praise indeed.

In the second set, however, Williams suddenly appeared unable to cope with the weight of her opponent's shots. Growing in confidence, Muguruza raised her level. The Spaniard, like many modern-day players, is most comfortable rallying from the baseline, but she also appreciates the value of coming forward and can volley beautifully. From being a player who felt uncomfortable on grass when she first played on it in 2012, she has grown to love the surface and to appreciate that it brings the best out of her. A double fault gave Muguruza a break in the first game of the second set, a missed volley put her 3-0 up and the Spaniard's backhand winner in the fifth game gave her the chance to serve out for the match.

Williams said afterwards that Muguruza had "competed really well" but was disappointed with her own performance. "There were errors and you can't make them," she said. "I went for some big shots and they didn't land."

Muguruza's display underlined her reputation as a big-occasion player. This was only her seventh singles final, but three of them have been in Grand Slam tournaments. "I always come very motivated to the Grand Slams," Muguruza said. "I came here thinking: 'I'm prepared, I feel good.' During the tournament and the matches, I was feeling better and better. Every match, I was increasing my level."

An amazing two decades since she first competed at Wimbledon as a teenager, 37-year-old Venus Williams appeared on Centre Court for her ninth Wimbledon final

Far left: Garbiñe Muguruza was in the form of her life as she powered to her second Grand Slam title, just over a year since she won the French Open by beating Venus' sister, Serena

Left: After the most unusual way to win her Championship point – by a successful appeal to Hawk-Eye – Muguruza slumped to her knees in elation

Below: After they had embraced at the net, Venus Williams later praised Muguruza for her performance: "I think she played amazing"

Between her triumphs at the 2016 French Open and The Championships 2017 Muguruza had not reached a single final. "People think that when you win it's so easy, but it's not easy to handle it," she said. "I probably always expect myself to play so well and when it doesn't happen it's hard to deal with. But the best way is to be humble and go back to the court, starting with the hard court season now. I'll keep working and things will come. But I'm not going to be thinking that I'm going to play incredible in every tournament."

The win took Muguruza up 10 places in the world to No.5, but she said that winning the biggest tournaments was more important to her than topping the rankings. "I don't know what it feels like to be number one, but I know what it feels like to win a Grand Slam and to win this trophy," she said.

The first player to beat both Williams sisters in Grand Slam finals, Muguruza was only the second Spaniard to win the ladies' title. The first, in 1994, was Conchita Martinez, who was helping Muguruza in the temporary absence of her regular coach, Sam Sumyk. Martinez saw parallels with her own triumph 23 years earlier. At 37 Williams was the oldest Wimbledon finalist since Martina Navratilova, who had been 230 days older when she lost to Martinez in the 1994 final. Two months before The Championships 23 years ago Martinez had beaten Navratilova on clay in Rome, which was where Muguruza beat Williams – for the first time – in 2017.

As Muguruza reflected on her triumph later in the evening, she talked about her love-hate relationship with tennis. "It's hard in defeat but it's very nice when you win," she said. "When you win everything is beautiful and when you lose everything is darker."

Muguruza, who was born and brought up in Venezuela but moved to Spain with her parents when she was six, admitted that she struggles to cope when she falls out of love with tennis. "I am still searching for that," she said. "It is hard because I've played since I was three years old and everything is tennis, tennis. I'm super-passionate about it and I love it. But I always like to cook, I like music, and I just try to be like a regular girl or woman."

The day concluded with the finals of the gentlemen's and ladies' doubles, which were very different matches. Poland's Lukasz Kubot and Brazil's Marcelo Melo beat Oliver Marach and Mate Pavic 5-7, 7-5, 7-6(2), 3-6, 13-11 after four hours and 40 minutes before Ekaterina Makarova and Elena Vesnina brushed aside Chan Hao-Ching and Monica Niculescu 6-0, 6-0 in just 55 minutes.

The Gentlemen's Doubles Final was tight from start to finish, with just six breaks of serve in total. Kubot and Melo failed to take two match points in the 12th game of the deciding set but broke to love in the 24th thanks to some scorching returns, after which Kubot celebrated with his customary display of can-can kicks while Melo lay horizontal on the turf. The Pole was appearing at his 12th Wimbledon and the Brazilian at his 11th, but for both men this was a first triumph at The Championships. Melo had lost

Previous pages: Muguruza posed for the traditional post-victory photo shoot with the Venus Rosewater Dish to warm applause on Centre Court

Above: The two finalists received the familiar guard of honour from the Ball Boys and Girls as they bade farewell to Centre Court

Opposite: The new champion presents the Venus Rosewater Dish to the crowds that have gathered beneath Centre Court's Members' Balcony

CHAMPION!

This watch is a witness to an amazing triumph at one of tennis's most prestigious events. Worn by a player whose remarkable persistence, elegance and power game have earned her a place among the sport's top players. Rolex congratulates Garbiñe Muguruza on her second Grand Slam® victory and first on grass at The Championships, Wimbledon. It doesn't just tell time. It tells history.

OYSTER PERPETUAL DATEJUST 36

VIVA ESPANA

Garbiñe Muguruza revealed before the Ladies' Singles Final that whenever she was in the vicinity of the Honours Board she could never resist gazing at the names of all those former champions and dreaming of how her name might one day fit there.

As well as noting quite how many times the names of the Williams sisters appeared – 12 times in 17 years between 2000 and 2016 – it also informed her that the last and only Spanish holder of the Venus Rosewater Dish was her coaching adviser, Conchita Martinez, back in 1994.

Watched by King Juan Carlos I, the former monarch of Spain, and his wife Queen Sofia, as well as some of her great predecessors like Martinez, the 1966 Gentlemen's Singles champion Manuel Santana, and two-time ladies' singles finalist Arantxa Sanchez Vicario, Muguruza played a dazzling match against Venus Williams to become only the fourth Spanish singles winner in Wimbledon history (the other being, of course, Rafael Nadal).

Muguruza explained that her Fed Cup captain Martinez – who was her chief training adviser during The Championships while her coach Sam Sumyk was back home with his heavily pregnant wife – had been a calming influence on her during the campaign, which was quite ironic considering how Conchita understandably became a bundle of nerves every time she was in the players' box watching her charge.

Amid all the excitement of her victory, Muguruza, in a quieter moment on Centre Court, couldn't resist balancing the Venus Rosewater Dish on her head so that it looked for all the world like a gold-and-silver sombrero.

It seemed an enjoyably fitting image on a day when the Centre Court had a particularly Latin feel and tennis could once again celebrate the reign of Spain.

Clockwise from top: Conchita Martinez is all smiles following her fellow Spaniard's victory; Juan Carlos I and his wife Sofia watched from the Royal Box; Muguruza joins her coaching adviser on the Honours Board

High-stepping epic

The Gentlemen's Doubles Final, which ended in floodlit excitement under the Centre Court roof just before 9pm, will go down as one of the more memorable – a four hours and 40 minutes epic in which Poland's Lukasz Kubot and Brazil's Marcelo Melo finally prevailed 13-11 in the fifth set against Austrian Oliver Marach and Croatian Mate Pavic.

As the fifth set rolled on with darkness falling, and with the Centre Court crowd anticipating an all-nighter as both pairs refused to give an inch, the decision was made to close the roof and finish the match indoors under lights. At 11-11, Kubot and Melo finally forced the crucial break, paving the way for a richly deserved victory that earned a standing ovation from the assembled spectators.

It will also live long in the memory for the ecstatic scenes that followed, particularly the exuberant celebrations of Kubot, who unleashed – to much amusement – his famous high-stepping dance across the court.

Lukasz Kubot was able to tap into his very last reserves of energy to round off a spectacular evening's entertainment with his unique victory celebration

his only previous final to the Bryan brothers in 2013 when playing with Ivan Dodig. The 33-year-old, for whom victory meant a return to No.1 in the men's doubles world rankings, said he had told Kubot before the match: "I did everything in my life to be here in this court. I want to enjoy it as much as I can. I reached the final once before but now I want to win – and I can do it."

Because of fading light the Centre Court roof was shut towards the end of the match, which finished just before 9pm. However, any fears that the ensuing Ladies' Doubles Final would not be over before the cut-off time of 11pm were promptly ended when Makarova and Vesnina completed the first 'double-bagel' victory in a Ladies' Doubles Final since 1953. The Russians, who won the French Open in 2013 and the US Open in 2014 before adding the Olympic title in 2016, were the perfect combination. Makarova hit some huge shots from the baseline while Vesnina dominated at the net. Vesnina said their victory was "very special" and thanked the crowd. "I know it was a long day today," she beamed happily. "But people in London, people in Wimbledon, they really appreciate every day. They come here every day. It's fully packed, every court."

Diede de Groot won her first Grand Slam title when she beat Germany's Sabine Ellerbrock 6-0, 6-4 in the final of the Ladies' Wheelchair Singles. The only time the Dutchwoman faltered was when she served for the match at 5-3, but after tightening up in that game she recovered to hit four clean winners in the next to secure her victory. "When I get nervous I just step off the aggressive game," de Groot said afterwards. "At 5-4 I tried to stay relaxed and go back to my own shots." Britain's Alfie Hewett and Gordon Reid successfully defended their Gentlemen's Wheelchair Doubles title, beating France's Stephane Houdet and Nicolas Peifer 6-7(5), 7-5, 7-6(3).

Claire Liu became the first American to win the girls' singles since 1992 when she beat Ann Li 6-2, 5-7, 6-2. The 17-year-old Californian, runner-up at the French Open a month earlier, failed to take three match points when she served at 5-4 and 40-0 in the second set, but held firm in the decider. "It feels amazing," she said afterwards. "I just keep smiling all the time. I still can't even believe it."

Gordon Reid (**left**) and Alfie Hewett became back-to-back Wimbledon champions in the Gentlemen's Wheelchair Doubles, defending their 2016 trophy with an exciting three-set win over French duo Stephane Houdet and Nicolas Peifer on No.3 Court

Dance fever

Olympic gold medallists and now Wimbledon champions, Russia's Elena Vesnina and Ekaterina Makarova are fast becoming one of the best – and most animated – double acts in tennis

● **Ladies' Doubles champions Elena Vesnina and Ekaterina Makarova** celebrated winning their third Grand Slam title together in animated fashion, bouncing up and down on Centre Court and high-fiving in delight after feeding Monica Niculescu and Chan Hao-Ching a 6-0, 6-0 'double bagel'.

They weren't always as effervescent as this though, revealed Vesnina, until they were en route to winning gold together in the 2016 Rio de Janeiro Olympics and found themselves inspired by watching other sports: "Before we were more quiet in doubles, even when we were celebrating our points; now we're more loud. We were watching volleyball in the Olympics and they were celebrating every match, hugging each other. I was like, 'We have to do that!'"

● **Garbiñe Muguruza couldn't help but protest** when she was asked after her wonderful ladies' singles triumph which of the two gentlemen's singles finalists she would most like to dance with – Marin Cilic or Roger Federer – as was once the tradition at Sunday night's Champions' Dinner.

"Aw, c'mon," she said, thinking how unfair the question was. Yet after a pause, she just broke into a big smile and blurted out: "Roger!" The Spaniard went on to explain: "I like Cilic, I have to say. But I want to see if Roger's also that elegant while dancing!"

● **Claire Liu, the new girls' singles champion**, hails from the city of Thousand Oaks in California – and the teenage US prospect didn't have to look very far to find real inspiration.

Californian teenager Claire Liu, the first American to lift the girls' singles trophy at Wimbledon since Chanda Rubin in 1992, found inspiration from another US player

Sam Querrey, the man who knocked out reigning Wimbledon champions Novak Djokovic and Andy Murray in successive years, also hails from the city just outside Los Angeles and is based at the same training facility at California State University.

"I see him training a lot. Definitely he's a great role model to look up to because he just works so hard," enthused Liu, while Querrey himself applauded the 17-year-old with the observation: "I probably see her 50 times a year, so I'm stoked for her. She's really good!"

● **Wimbledon towels have always been a must-have item** for players and supporters alike, but none will have been coveted quite like the special ones presented to this year's finalists. For the first time, all finalists in 2017 had two personalised towels created for them to mark the occasion, with their names embroidered into the fabric. True collectors' items.

DAY
13
SUNDAY
16 JULY

Roger Federer had been here before. In both 2014 and 2015 the Swiss had been on the brink of becoming the most successful male player in the history of The Championships, only to have his dreams dashed in the final by the brilliance of Novak Djokovic.

After the second of those defeats, even the most devoted of Federer fans must have wondered whether he was destined to remain forever bracketed with William Renshaw and Pete Sampras as the only players to win the gentlemen's singles title seven times. Renshaw, in 1889, and Sampras, in 2000, had both won their last singles titles at the All England Club when they were 28; Federer was 33 and had won only one Grand

Slam tournament – at Wimbledon in 2012 – in the last five-and-a-half-years.

If Federer's chances of moving past Renshaw and Sampras appeared to be receding in 2015, they were perhaps looking even bleaker by the time he boarded a plane for Australia at the end of 2016 after a six-month break from competition. Dogged by knee and back problems, the former world No.1 had called an end to his 2016 season after losing in the Wimbledon semi-finals. By the time The Championships 2017 came around he would be a month short of his 36th birthday.

Most seasoned Federer watchers have learned never to write off the player widely acclaimed as the greatest in tennis history, but surely nobody – not even the man himself – could have predicted what would happen next. If his victory at the Australian Open in January 2017 had not been astonishing enough, here he was now just one win away from what would be the ultimate triumph of his extraordinary career. At 35 years and 342 days he was the oldest gentlemen's singles finalist at The Championships since Ken Rosewall in 1974; with victory he would become the oldest man to win the title in the Open era. And, at long last, the first man to win it eight times.

With due respect to Marin Cilic, who had won the US Open three years earlier and had been in fine form on grass, Federer may have been relieved that he was not facing a member of the so-called 'Big Four', as he had in all seven of the Grand Slam finals he had contested since 2009. Between them, Federer, Djokovic, Rafael Nadal and Andy Murray had won every Wimbledon title from 2003 onwards.

Previous pages: All hail the conquering hero. Roger Federer salutes his Centre Court disciples after winning a record eighth Wimbledon gentlemen's singles title

Left: Marin Cilic failed in his bid to become only the second Croatian man to win the Gentlemen's Singles Final after Goran Ivanisevic, the champion in 2001

Cilic, whose only victory in seven previous meetings with Federer had been en route to his US Open title, had been on court for almost 14-and-a-half hours in his first six matches and had come through bruising marathons in his last two, against Gilles Muller and Sam Querrey. Federer, looking as fresh as ever, had been in action for less than 10 hours in total, having not dropped a set.

One hour and 41 minutes after Cilic got the 131st Gentlemen's Singles Final under way, that record was still intact. Federer had always been most experts' favourite to beat the 28-year-old Croat, but few would have guessed at the manner of his triumph. Federer's swift 6-3, 6-1, 6-4 victory was his biggest winning margin in his eight Wimbledon finals.

By the middle of the second set Cilic was sobbing into his towel at a changeover, his chances having been dashed by a painful blister on his left foot that had first troubled him during his victory over Querrey. "Every time that I had to do a fast reaction, a fast change of movement, I was unable to do that," Cilic said after the final. "It was actually very difficult to focus on the match, as well. My mind was blocked with the pain all the time. It was tough for me to focus on the tactics, on the things that I needed to do."

At 35 years and 342 days, Roger Federer became the oldest man in the Open era to win the Wimbledon singles title

Nevertheless, until Federer started to run away with the match in the second set there had been few early indications that Cilic had a problem. On a warm and muggy day, both men had quickly found their stride. Cilic failed to convert what proved to be his only break point of the match in the fourth game and then dropped serve at 2-2. Federer, one of the best frontrunners, took the opening set in 36 minutes by breaking Cilic again, the world No.6 double-faulting on set point.

Federer, who in playing his 102nd match at The Championships equalled Jimmy Connors' Open era men's record, was soon 3-0 up in the second set, upon which Cilic called for the doctor and trainer at a changeover, during which he seemed inconsolable. Might this be the first retirement in a Gentlemen's Singles Final for 106 years, onlookers wondered? Cilic, however, soldiered on before taking a medical time-out for treatment at the end of the second set. His level picked up in the third, but at 3-3 Federer broke again. The Swiss served out for his victory, which he completed on his second match point with his eighth ace.

Federer, who made only eight unforced errors to Cilic's 23, said afterwards that he had been unaware of the nature of his opponent's problem. "He was serving big," Federer said. "He was serve-and-volleying. So I guessed movement for that reason wasn't the biggest problem, maybe. When he called the doctor at first I thought maybe he was dizzy or something. Because I couldn't tell what it was, it actually made things easier. I just said to myself: 'Focus on your game, focus on your match, keep playing.' The good thing is I was already in the lead."

Cilic described his defeat as "devastating" but said he would take heart from his performances over the whole Fortnight. "I know that these last two weeks have been great tennis from me," he said. "My level was in a position where it hasn't been before on grass, so I'm extremely satisfied with that, extremely happy. This will give me much more confidence, much more strength for the rest of the year."

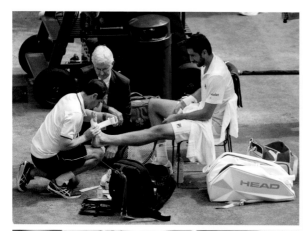

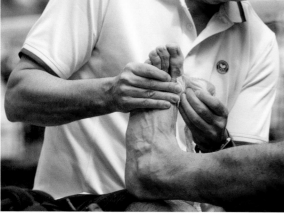

Federer's 93rd singles title was his 19th at Grand Slam level, which put him four clear of Nadal on the all-time list of men's champions. Only Margaret Court (24 titles), Serena Williams (23) and Steffi Graf (22) have won more. Federer's fifth title of the year also put him one ahead of second-placed Nadal on the 2017 list as the two men continued their remarkable hold on the season's major honours. This was the fifth time – but the first since 2010 – that the Swiss and the Spaniard had between them won the first three Grand Slam titles of the year. With Nadal having won his tenth French Open a month earlier, Federer became only the second man ever to win the same Grand Slam title at least eight times.

Federer said it was "very special" to break the record of gentlemen's singles titles at The Championships. "Wimbledon was always my favourite tournament and will always be my favourite tournament," he said. "My heroes walked the grounds here and walked the courts here. Because of them, I think I became a better player, too. To mark history here at Wimbledon really means a lot to me just because of all of that. It's that simple."

The Swiss said he was "incredibly surprised" at how the year had turned out. "I knew I could do great again maybe one day, but not at this level," he said. "I guess you would have laughed, too, if I had told you I was going to win two Slams this year. People wouldn't believe me if I said that. I also didn't believe that I was going to win two this year. It's incredible."

Federer said he expected to be back to defend his title in 2018, though he said there was "never a guarantee", especially at his age. At the Champions' Dinner in London's Guildhall later that evening, Philip Brook, the Chairman of the All England Club, paid tribute to Federer's "unbelievably outstanding achievement". He presented the champion with a framed photographic montage of his eight triumphs on Centre Court. Federer, clutching the Wimbledon trophy, said he used to think it would be "absolutely impossible" to beat the record of Sampras, who had been his hero. Now he had done so, it seemed "surreal".

There was nothing but sadness for Marin Čilić, who said his tears in the final had stemmed from the injury leading to "a feeling that I knew that I cannot give my best tennis on the court"

Right: Roger Federer has a bigger army of fans than any other player – as you could gather from the sea of red atop The Hill watching the match on the Big Screen – some of whom hoisted aloft the numbers eight and 19 the moment Federer won his record eighth gentlemen's singles title and 19th Grand Slam (**below**)

Opposite: "I've done it!" Federer finally surpasses William Renshaw and Pete Sampras at SW19

Right: Marin Čilić received a sympathetic and heartfelt ovation from the crowd as he lifted aloft his salver

Opposite: A delighted Federer holds aloft an old friend – the Challenge Cup

On the screen above the stage there were photographs of Federer hiking in the Swiss Alps during last year's US Open. "For people who don't know what to do in the next few weeks and months, this is the place to go to," he said with a smile. "It gives you incredible energy for the next year."

Standing alongside Garbiñe Muguruza, Federer congratulated the Spaniard on her "absolutely stunning" victory in the ladies' singles. "Winning Wimbledon, you're a Wimbledon champion for life," Federer said. "To be part of Wimbledon history is something that is very special to me and I'm sure it's going to be special for you too in the coming years."

When he returned to the All England Club the next morning Federer admitted that his head was still ringing following his celebrations, which had continued long into the night. Asked what his next goals were, he replied: "The target now is to enjoy being Wimbledon champion for a year."

After Federer's victory there was still time on Centre Court for another Swiss triumph as Martina Hingis partnered Britain's Jamie Murray to victory in the mixed doubles to claim her 23rd Grand Slam title. The No.1 seeds beat the defending champions, Finland's Henri Kontinen and Britain's Heather Watson, 6-4, 6-4 in the final. Murray, who had won the title on one previous occasion, with Jelena Jankovic in 2007, was outstanding at the net, while Hingis hit some excellent returns. With Britons on both sides of the net most of the crowd seemed to find it hard to take sides. One spectator summed up the general feeling when he called out: "Come on all of you!"

Murray had not been planning to play in the mixed doubles until he received a call from Hingis, who had split with Leander Paes. "I probably would have said no to anyone else, but Martina called and it was a good decision," he said. Hingis added: "I am really happy I decided to contact Jamie before Wimbledon and I am also very happy it was my British player that won the trophy." She thought she and Murray had good chemistry on court. "We know where we stand, what we do, what we can expect from one another as doubles players," Hingis said.

"A WONDERFUL MOMENT FOR US AS A FAMILY"

Roger Federer broke a whole host of records by winning his eighth Wimbledon gentlemen's singles crown. Some of them may eventually be broken one day, but we would like to hazard a fair guess that no one will ever repeat his achievement of being the champion who won while also being the father of two sets of twins.

The scene of the young Federers – seven-year-old daughters Myla Rose and Charlene Riva and three-year-old sons Leo and Lenny – with their mother Mirka and grandmother Lynette after being brought into the players' box for the trophy presentation was a unique and delightful sight.

"They have no clue what's going on, they think this is probably a nice view and a nice playground," smiled Federer on court as he glanced up to see the boys dangling their legs over the edge of the box after the match. "One day, hopefully, they'll understand. It's very special. It's a wonderful moment for us as a family."

It certainly was. Asked what kept him going in the sport, he had a special tribute for his wife, Mirka. "My wife's totally fine with me still playing," he said. "She's my number one supporter. She's amazing!" That's both of them then…

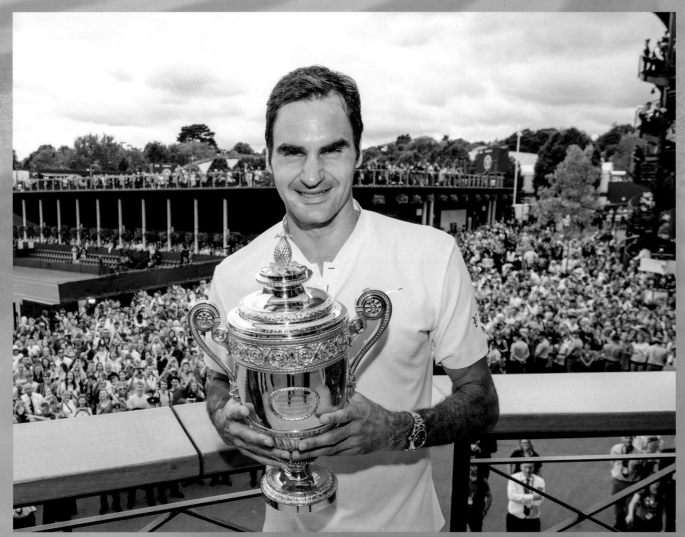

"I'm not finished yet"

If we all thought Roger Federer winning the gentlemen's singles at 35 was incredible enough, the maestro had everyone's heart racing afterwards when he contemplated the unreal prospect of being back at SW19 not just for another year – but perhaps even when he was 40.

"I don't know how much longer it's going to last. I have no idea," pondered Federer, as he talked of whether he would be able to maintain the wondrous form that had seen him lose just two out of 33 matches during the first half of 2017. "I've just got to always remind myself that health comes first at this point. If I do that, maybe things are actually possible I didn't think were."

Like playing until he was 40? "I mean, you would think so, if your health is permitting and everything is okay," he replied. How would he keep himself in sufficient shape at that age? "You could take 300 days off beforehand, just prepare for Wimbledon and put yourself in a freeze box," he smiled. "Then you come out and train a bit, you know you're not going to be injured."

Maybe Federer had discovered the secret to success as a 30-something – that less is somehow more – a practice the Williams sisters have sometimes demonstrated, in fact. "I feel like I'm working part-time these days almost, which is a great feeling," he smiled, after seeing his name written on the Honours Board for a record-breaking eighth time.

And his audience dissolved into laughter as the great man pondered aloud why he had played so well after having had six months away from the game in 2016 recuperating before electing to also miss the entire 2017 clay court season. "I've gotta take more time off," he mused with a smile.

Sweden's Stefan Olsson won his first Grand Slam singles title in his third final when he beat Argentina's Gustavo Fernandez 7-5, 3-6, 7-5 in the Gentlemen's Wheelchair Singles. Fernandez actually led 5-3 in each set, but Olsson's clever use of slice proved crucial. "It's the best feeling in the world," Olsson said afterwards. "Before this I'd won a gold medal at the Paralympics, but this beats it by a mile – by 500,000 miles maybe." Britain's Jordanne Whiley and Japan's Yui Kamiji won the Ladies' Wheelchair Doubles title for the fourth year in a row but had to come from a set behind in the final to do so. They eventually beat the Netherlands' Marjolein Buis and Diede de Groot 2-6, 6-3, 6-0. After The Championships Whiley revealed that she had been 11 weeks pregnant during the final.

Twenty-four hours after Muguruza's triumph, another Spaniard tasted success by winning the boys' singles title. Alejandro Davidovich Fokina, who beat Argentina's Axel Geller 7-6(2), 6-3 in the final, became only the second Spaniard to win the junior title following Manuel Orantes' success in 1967. Geller, who had beaten the No.1 seed, Corentin Moutet, in the semi-finals and hit one serve timed at 135mph, took a medical time-out because of a back problem early in the second set. Geller and Chinese Taipei's Hsu Yu Hsiou beat Austria's Jurij Rodionov and the Czech Republic's Michael Vrbensky 6-4, 6-4 to win the boys' doubles title. The girls' doubles was won by Serbia's Olga Danilovic and Slovenia's Kaja Juvan, who beat the Americans Catherine McNally and Whitney Osuigwe 6-4, 6-3 in the final.

For all of the champions, the past 13 days had provided personal memories to treasure for a lifetime. Along with everyone else who had been at the All England Club over the previous two weeks, they could also cherish the thought that they had been part of a Championships that would go down in history thanks to the achievements of one man, the incomparable Roger Federer.

Jordanne Whiley and Yui Kamiji believe the secret of their brilliant partnership is that they're the very best of friends, and that chemistry was evident again as they won a fourth successive Ladies' Wheelchair Doubles title against Marjolein Buis and Diede de Groot

Double the fun

As Jamie Murray and Swiss great Martina Hingis (*above*) won the mixed doubles title against defending champions Heather Watson and Finland's Henri Kontinen (*right*), it wasn't just the delightful novelty of a Wimbledon final featuring a British player on either side of the net that made the occasion such a treat. It was also that the simple pleasure all the players displayed seemed to rub off on the whole Centre Court crowd, who were caught up in the cheery spirit of the occasion.

"It's easy to play with Martina. She's always smiling and happy which makes it easy for me," said Murray, after marvelling how Hingis had picked up a remarkable 23rd Grand Slam title in both singles and doubles.

The pair had smiles on their faces throughout the tournament, evidently savouring just how their partnership had gelled so quickly after Hingis had made a hopeful request to Murray in the build-up to Wimbledon. In her own laughing words, she had asked him by text: "Hi, Jamie, want to play with me?" To which, of course, Murray could only have one possible answer. "I'm not used to 'no'," explained Martina with a big smile.

THE LAWN TENNIS CHAMPIONSHIPS
GENTLEMEN'S SINGLES

1937	J.D. Bud...
1938	J.D. Bud...
1939	R.L.Rig...
1946	Y. Pet...
1947	J...
1948	...

1971	J.D. Newcombe
1972	S.R. Smith
1973	J. Kodes
1974	J.S. Connors
1975	A.R. Ashe
1976	B. Borg
1977	B. Borg
1978	B. Borg
1979	B. Borg
1980	B. Borg
1981	J.P. McEnroe
1982	J.S. Connors
1983	J.P. McEnroe
1984	J.P. McEnroe
	B. Becker
	B. Becker
	P. Cash
	. Edberg
	. Becker
	Edberg
	Stich
	Agassi
	ampras
	ampras

1999	P. Sampras
2000	P. Sampras
2001	G. Ivanisevic
2002	L. Hewitt
2003	**R. Federer**
2004	**R. Federer**
2005	**R. Federer**
2006	**R. Federer**
2007	R. Federer
2008	R. Nadal
2009	R. Federer
2010	R. Nadal
2011	N. Djokovic
2012	R. Federer
2013	A. Murray
2014	N. Djokovic
2015	N. Djokovic
2016	A. Murray
2017	R. Federer

Eighth time's the charm

Roger Federer, accompanied by the All England Club Chairman Philip Brook, was thrilled to see his name on the Honours Board yet again

CHAMPIONSHIPS Day 13 NOTEBOOK

● **There was something eerily magical about the number eight** for Roger Federer at these Championships. After the Swiss' Gentlemen's Singles Final triumph the statistical wizards of wimbledon.com noted that the man born on the eighth day of the eighth month had won his eighth Wimbledon title with his eighth ace of the match in his eighth meeting with Marin Cilic, having lost just eight games in the final. Spooky.

● **The BBC seemed determined to make sure** that the last Sunday of The Championships 2017 was as action-packed as possible. Viewers got to watch Roger Federer – a timeless lord if ever there was one – on Centre Court before a new Time Lord, Doctor Who, was revealed to the public later that evening. It felt rather appropriate then that David Tennant, a previous incarnation of the Doctor, should be in the Royal Box to see Federer defy the march of time yet again.

● **You could hardly imagine a more starry cast** than the one that lined up to applaud the 2017 Gentlemen's Singles champion as he made his way from Centre Court to the South West Hall Balcony to show off the Challenge Cup to his fans below.
Federer was congratulated by a crowd that included the Duke and Duchess of Cambridge, Prince Albert of Monaco and a host of former Wimbledon champions. One of those champions, American legend

Stan Smith, asked Federer amid all the fuss: "How does it feel?" to which the great man shrugged with a smile: "Still the same..."

● **There wasn't a person at Wimbledon not impacted** in some way by Federer's achievement. Even the new boys' singles champion, Alejandro Davidovich Fokina, who wasn't even born when the Swiss won the same title in 1998, remembered how Federer was his first idol, the one whose feats

Alejandro Davidovich Fokina was just one of many young players to be inspired by Federer

pushed him to play tennis when he was growing up. "I cried with Roger when he won the Grand Slam," the 18-year-old Spaniard recalled.

● **It says much about Federer's popularity** that even his fellow players seemed in awe of him at the Champions' Dinner. As Elena Vesnina told reporters: "Roger was in high demand. The second he was standing up from his chair and going somewhere, somebody would come to him. Even players were coming and asking for photos!
"He has always been the most popular player on the tour. Every time he enters the locker room it gets silent and people only look at him. He is a huge star, but he never shows that he is. He is very down to earth, gallant and careful. He is respectful with people, it doesn't matter if it's tournament staff or other players."
The best tribute of all, really.

The Champions' Dinner

Roger Federer and Garbiñe Muguruza were the centre of attention at the Champions' Dinner, just as they had been on Centre Court with their glorious victories over the Finals weekend.

Muguruza told the audience at London's Guildhall that she'd been in such shock after her success on Saturday that she'd barely been able to sleep. Then, only when she awoke on Sunday after catching just a few winks, she was able to pinch herself and think: "It's true – I made it!"

Having presented Federer with a specially framed montage of photographs of his gentlemen's singles triumphs, All England Club Chairman Philip Brook suggested there was room for more photos at the bottom. "It's just a totally different time to 2003," responded Federer as he reflected on his incredible career. "Fourteen years ago I was a different man. It definitely never grows old, winning Wimbledon."

WIMBLEDON 2017

The Gentlemen's Singles

 **Roger FEDERER**

The Ladies' Singles

 **Garbiñe MUGURUZA**

The Gentlemen's Doubles

 **Lukasz KUBOT** **Marcelo MELO**

The Ladies' Doubles

 **Ekaterina MAKAROVA** **Elena VESNINA**

The Mixed Doubles

 **Jamie MURRAY** **Martina HINGIS**

THE CHAMPIONS

The Boys' Singles

Alejandro DAVIDOVICH FOKINA

The Girls' Singles

Claire LIU

The Boys' Doubles

Hsu Yu HSIOU Axel GELLER

The Girls' Doubles

Olga DANILOVIC Kaja JUVAN

The Gentlemen's Invitation Doubles

Lleyton HEWITT Mark PHILIPPOUSSIS

The Ladies' Invitation Doubles

Martina NAVRATILOVA Cara BLACK

The Senior Gentlemen's Invitation Doubles

Jacco ELTINGH Paul HAARHUIS

The Gentlemen's Wheelchair Singles

Stefan OLSSON

The Ladies' Wheelchair Singles

Diede DE GROOT

The Gentlemen's Wheelchair Doubles

Gordon REID Alfie HEWETT

The Ladies' Wheelchair Doubles

Jordanne WHILEY Yui KAMIJI

EVENT 1 – THE GENTLEMEN'S SINGLES CHAMPIONSHIP 2017

Holder: ANDY MURRAY (GBR)

The Champion will become the holder, for the year only, of the CHALLENGE CUP presented by The All England Lawn Tennis and Croquet Club in 1887. The Champion will receive a silver three-quarter size replica of the Challenge Cup. A Silver Salver will be presented to the Runner-up and a Bronze Medal to each defeated semi-finalist. The matches will be the best of five sets.

First Round

	No.	Player	Country
	1.	**Andy Murray [1]** *(1)*	(GBR)
(LL)	2.	Alexander Bublik *(135)*	(KAZ)
	3.	Joao Sousa *(62)*	(POR)
	4.	Dustin Brown *(97)*	(GER)
	5.	Jiri Vesely *(48)*	(CZE)
(Q)	6.	Illya Marchenko *(117)*	(UKR)
	7.	Dmitry Tursunov *(89)*	(RUS)
	8.	**Fabio Fognini [28]** *(29)*	(ITA)
	9.	**Nick Kyrgios [20]** *(20)*	(AUS)
	10.	Pierre-Hugues Herbert *(70)*	(FRA)
	11.	Rogerio Dutra Silva *(69)*	(BRA)
	12.	Benoit Paire *(46)*	(FRA)
(WC)	13.	Denis Shapovalov *(164)*	(CAN)
	14.	Jerzy Janowicz *(94)*	(POL)
	15.	Malek Jaziri *(77)*	(TUN)
	16.	**Lucas Pouille [14]** *(16)*	(FRA)
	17.	**Jo-Wilfried Tsonga [12]** *(10)*	(FRA)
(WC)	18.	Cameron Norrie *(221)*	(GBR)
(Q)	19.	Simone Bolelli *(313)*	(ITA)
	20.	Yen-Hsun Lu *(75)*	(TPE)
	21.	Carlos Berlocq *(80)*	(ARG)
	22.	Nikoloz Basilashvili *(54)*	(GEO)
	23.	Thomas Fabbiano *(91)*	(ITA)
	24.	**Sam Querrey [24]** *(28)*	(USA)
	25.	**Fernando Verdasco [31]** *(35)*	(ESP)
	26.	Kevin Anderson *(42)*	(RSA)
	27.	Norbert Gombos *(93)*	(SVK)
	28.	Andreas Seppi *(87)*	(ITA)
(WC)	29.	Tommy Haas *(258)*	(GER)
(Q)	30.	Ruben Bemelmans *(124)*	(BEL)
	31.	Daniil Medvedev *(49)*	(RUS)
	32.	**Stan Wawrinka [5]** *(3)*	(SUI)
	33.	**Rafael Nadal [4]** *(2)*	(ESP)
	34.	John Millman *(81)*	(AUS)
	35.	Donald Young *(43)*	(USA)
	36.	Denis Istomin *(72)*	(UZB)
	37.	Thiago Monteiro *(100)*	(BRA)
(Q)	38.	Andrew Whittington *(211)*	(AUS)
	39.	Andrey Kuznetsov *(76)*	(RUS)
	40.	**Karen Khachanov [30]** *(34)*	(RUS)
	41.	**Ivo Karlovic [21]** *(23)*	(CRO)
	42.	Aljaz Bedene *(58)*	(GBR)
	43.	Damir Dzumhur *(83)*	(BIH)
	44.	Renzo Olivo *(89)*	(ARG)
(Q)	45.	Lukas Rosol *(215)*	(CZE)
	46.	Henri Laaksonen *(104)*	(SUI)
(WC)	47.	Marton Fucsovics *(109)*	(HUN)
	48.	**Gilles Muller [16]** *(26)*	(LUX)
	49.	**Kei Nishikori [9]** *(9)*	(JPN)
	50.	Marco Cecchinato *(102)*	(ITA)
	51.	Julien Benneteau *(81)*	(FRA)
(Q)	52.	Sergiy Stakhovsky *(122)*	(UKR)
(Q)	53.	Peter Gojowczyk *(140)*	(GER)
	54.	Marius Copil *(85)*	(ROU)
	55.	Andreas Haider-Maurer *(63)*	(AUT)
	56.	**Roberto Bautista Agut [18]** *(19)*	(ESP)
	57.	**Steve Johnson [26]** *(31)*	(USA)
	58.	Nicolas Kicker *(94)*	(ARG)
	59.	Facundo Bagnis *(107)*	(ARG)
	60.	Radu Albot *(108)*	(MDA)
	61.	Viktor Troicki *(40)*	(SRB)
	62.	Florian Mayer *(114)*	(GER)
	63.	Philipp Kohlschreiber *(60)*	(GER)
	64.	**Marin Cilic [7]** *(6)*	(CRO)
	65.	**Milos Raonic [6]** *(7)*	(CAN)
	66.	Jan-Lennard Struff *(53)*	(GER)
	67.	Mikhail Youzhny *(82)*	(RUS)
	68.	Nicolas Mahut *(78)*	(FRA)
(Q)	69.	Andrey Rublev *(95)*	(RUS)
(Q)	70.	Stefano Travaglia *(155)*	(ITA)
	71.	Jordan Thompson *(86)*	(AUS)
	72.	**Albert Ramos-Vinolas [25]** *(22)*	(ESP)
	73.	**Jack Sock [17]** *(18)*	(USA)
(Q)	74.	Christian Garin *(220)*	(CHI)
	75.	Thomaz Bellucci *(55)*	(BRA)
(Q)	76.	Sebastian Ofner *(217)*	(AUT)
	77.	Robin Haase *(38)*	(NED)
	78.	Frances Tiafoe *(64)*	(USA)
	79.	Evgeny Donskoy *(98)*	(RUS)
	80.	**Alexander Zverev [10]** *(12)*	(GER)
	81.	**Grigor Dimitrov [13]** *(11)*	(BUL)
	82.	Diego Schwartzman *(37)*	(ARG)
(WC)	83.	James Ward *(1085)*	(GBR)
	84.	Marcos Baghdatis *(65)*	(CYP)
	85.	Dudi Sela *(90)*	(ISR)
	86.	Marcel Granollers *(112)*	(ESP)
(Q)	87.	Taylor Fritz *(128)*	(USA)
	88.	**John Isner [23]** *(21)*	(USA)
	89.	**Mischa Zverev [27]** *(30)*	(GER)
	90.	Bernard Tomic *(59)*	(AUS)
	91.	Mikhail Kukushkin *(118)*	(KAZ)
	92.	Taro Daniel *(92)*	(JPN)
(Q)	93.	Stefanos Tsitsipas *(192)*	(GRE)
	94.	Dusan Lajovic *(79)*	(SRB)
	95.	Alexandr Dolgopolov *(84)*	(UKR)
	96.	**Roger Federer [3]** *(5)*	(SUI)
	97.	**Dominic Thiem [8]** *(8)*	(AUT)
	98.	Vasek Pospisil *(73)*	(CAN)
	99.	Gilles Simon *(36)*	(FRA)
(Q)	100.	Nicolas Jarry *(182)*	(CHI)
	101.	Janko Tipsarevic *(63)*	(SRB)
	102.	Jared Donaldson *(67)*	(USA)
	103.	Horacio Zeballos *(52)*	(ARG)
	104.	**Paolo Lorenzi [32]** *(33)*	(ITA)
	105.	**Richard Gasquet [22]** *(27)*	(FRA)
	106.	David Ferrer *(39)*	(ESP)
	107.	Steve Darcis *(61)*	(BEL)
	108.	Ricardas Berankis *(93)*	(LTU)
	109.	Borna Coric *(45)*	(CRO)
	110.	Ryan Harrison *(41)*	(USA)
	111.	Jeremy Chardy *(71)*	(FRA)
	112.	**Tomas Berdych [11]** *(15)*	(CZE)
	113.	**Gael Monfils [15]** *(14)*	(FRA)
(Q)	114.	Daniel Brands *(216)*	(GER)
	115.	Kyle Edmund *(50)*	(GBR)
(Q)	116.	Alexander Ward *(869)*	(GBR)
	117.	Yuichi Sugita *(44)*	(JPN)
(WC)	118.	Brydan Klein *(232)*	(GBR)
	119.	Adrian Mannarino *(51)*	(FRA)
	120.	**Feliciano Lopez [19]** *(25)*	(ESP)
	121.	**Juan Martin Del Potro [29]** *(32)*	(ARG)
	122.	Thanasi Kokkinakis *(81)*	(AUS)
	123.	Ernests Gulbis *(99)*	(LAT)
	124.	Victor Estrella Burgos *(96)*	(DOM)
	125.	Adam Pavlasek *(136)*	(CZE)
	126.	Ernesto Escobedo *(74)*	(USA)
	127.	Martin Klizan *(47)*	(SVK)
	128.	**Novak Djokovic [2]** *(4)*	(SRB)

Second Round

Andy Murray [1]	6/1 6/4 6/2
Dustin Brown	3/6 7/6(5) 6/4 6/4
Jiri Vesely	6/1 4/6 4/6 7/5 6/1
Fabio Fognini [28]	6/1 6/3 6/3
Pierre-Hugues Herbert	6/3 6/4 0/0 Ret'd
Benoit Paire	6/4 3/6 7/6(10) 6/4
Jerzy Janowicz	6/4 3/6 6/3 7/6(2)
Lucas Pouille [14]	6/7(5) 6/4 6/4 7/6(2)
Jo-Wilfried Tsonga [12]	6/3 6/2 6/2
Simone Bolelli	6/3 1/6 6/3 6/4
Nikoloz Basilashvili	6/4 7/6(3) 6/1
Sam Querrey [24]	7/6(5) 7/5 6/2
Kevin Anderson	2/6 7/6(5) 7/6(8) 6/3
Andreas Seppi	6/2 3/6 6/2 6/1
Ruben Bemelmans	6/2 3/6 6/3 7/5
Daniil Medvedev	6/4 3/6 6/4 6/1
Rafael Nadal [4]	6/1 6/3 6/2
Donald Young	5/7 6/4 6/4 4/2 Ret'd
Thiago Monteiro	4/6 6/3 7/6(4) 7/6(5)
Karen Khachanov [30]	7/6(4) 2/6 6/3 1/6 6/2
Aljaz Bedene	6/7(5) 7/6(6) 6/7(7) 7/6(7) 8/6
Damir Dzumhur	6/2 6/0 6/1
Lukas Rosol	4/6 7/5 6/3 6/4
Gilles Muller [16]	7/5 6/4 6/2
Kei Nishikori [9]	6/2 6/2 6/0
Sergiy Stakhovsky	6/3 7/6(8) 2/6 6/2
Peter Gojowczyk	7/6(5) 2/6 6/3 6/1
Roberto Bautista Agut [18]	6/3 6/1 6/2
Steve Johnson [26]	6/4 7/5 6/3
Radu Albot	4/6 6/4 7/6(9) 7/6(3)
Florian Mayer	6/1 0/0 Ret'd
Marin Cilic [7]	6/4 6/2 6/3
Milos Raonic [6]	7/6(5) 6/2 7/6(4)
Mikhail Youzhny	6/2 7/5 6/4
Andrey Rublev	6/7(3) 6/3 7/5 1/6 7/5
Albert Ramos-Vinolas [25]	6/4 6/4 7/6(4)
Jack Sock [17]	6/3 4/6 7/6(4) 6/3
Sebastian Ofner	6/2 6/3 6/2
Frances Tiafoe	6/3 3/6 7/6(5) 7/5
Alexander Zverev [10]	6/4 7/6(3) 6/3
Grigor Dimitrov [13]	7/6(4) 6/2 6/2
Marcos Baghdatis	6/4 6/4 6/3
Dudi Sela	4/6 6/3 1/6 6/2 6/1
John Isner [23]	6/4 7/6(3) 6/3
Mischa Zverev [27]	6/4 6/3 6/4
Mikhail Kukushkin	4/6 6/4 7/6(4) 6/2
Dusan Lajovic	6/4 6/4 6/4
Roger Federer [3]	6/3 3/0 Ret'd
Dominic Thiem [8]	6/4 6/4 6/3
Gilles Simon	7/6(4) 6/3 6/3
Jared Donaldson	5/0 Ret'd
Paolo Lorenzi [32]	7/6(3) 4/6 7/6(8) 7/5
David Ferrer	6/3 6/4 5/7 6/2
Steve Darcis	4/6 6/3 2/6 6/4 6/3
Ryan Harrison	7/6(4) 6/4 7/6(6)
Tomas Berdych [11]	6/3 3/6 7/6(4) 6/4
Gael Monfils [15]	6/3 7/5 6/4
Kyle Edmund	4/6 6/3 6/2 6/1
Yuichi Sugita	7/6(5) 6/3 6/0
Adrian Mannarino	5/7 6/1 6/1 4/3 Ret'd
Juan Martin Del Potro [29]	6/3 3/6 7/6(2) 6/4
Ernests Gulbis	6/1 6/1 6/2
Adam Pavlasek	6/7(7) 6/1 6/3 6/1
Novak Djokovic [2]	6/3 2/0 Ret'd

Third Round

Andy Murray [1]	6/3 6/2 6/2
Fabio Fognini [28]	7/6(3) 6/4 6/2
Benoit Paire	7/6(4) 6/1 6/4
Jerzy Janowicz	7/6(4) 7/6(5) 3/6 6/1
Jo-Wilfried Tsonga [12]	6/1 7/5 6/2
Sam Querrey [24]	6/4 4/6 6/3 6/3
Kevin Anderson	6/3 7/6(4) 6/3
Ruben Bemelmans	6/4 6/2 3/6 2/6 6/3
Rafael Nadal [4]	6/4 6/2 7/5
Karen Khachanov [30]	3/6 7/6(5) 7/6(3) 7/5
Aljaz Bedene	6/3 3/6 6/3 6/3
Gilles Muller [16]	7/5 6/7(7) 4/6 6/3 9/7
Kei Nishikori [9]	6/4 6/7(7) 6/1 7/6(6)
Roberto Bautista Agut [18]	6/2 6/1 3/6 6/3
Steve Johnson [26]	6/3 6/3 4/6 6/3
Marin Cilic [7]	7/6(2) 6/4 7/5
Milos Raonic [6]	3/6 7/6(7) 6/4 7/5
Albert Ramos-Vinolas [25]	7/5 6/7(6) 4/6 6/3 6/4
Sebastian Ofner	6/3 6/4 3/6 2/6 6/2
Alexander Zverev [10]	6/3 6/4 6/3
Grigor Dimitrov [13]	6/3 6/2 6/1
Dudi Sela	6/7(5) 7/6(5) 5/7 7/6(5) 6/3
Mischa Zverev [27]	6/1 6/2 2/6 3/6 6/4
Roger Federer [3]	7/6(0) 6/3 6/2
Dominic Thiem [8]	5/7 6/4 6/2 6/4
Jared Donaldson	6/4 7/6(0) 6/7(0) 6/2
David Ferrer	3/0 Ret'd
Tomas Berdych [11]	6/4 6/3 6/7(8) 6/3
Gael Monfils [15]	7/6(1) 6/4 6/4
Adrian Mannarino	6/1 5/7 4/6 7/6(2) 6/2
Ernests Gulbis	6/4 6/4 7/6(3)
Novak Djokovic [2]	6/2 6/2 6/1

Fourth Round

Andy Murray [1]	6/2 4/6 6/1 7/5
Benoit Paire	6/2 7/6(3) 6/3
Sam Querrey [24]	6/2 3/6 7/6(5) 1/6 7/5
Kevin Anderson	7/6(3) 6/4 7/6(3)
Rafael Nadal [4]	6/1 6/4 7/6(3)
Gilles Muller [16]	7/6(4) 7/5 6/4
Roberto Bautista Agut [18]	6/4 7/6(3) 3/6 6/3
Marin Cilic [7]	6/4 7/6(3) 6/4
Milos Raonic [6]	7/6(3) 6/4 7/5
Alexander Zverev [10]	6/4 6/4 6/2
Grigor Dimitrov [13]	6/1 6/1 0/0 Ret'd
Roger Federer [3]	7/6(3) 6/4 6/4
Dominic Thiem [8]	7/5 6/4 6/2
Tomas Berdych [11]	6/3 6/4 6/3
Adrian Mannarino	7/6(3) 4/6 5/7 6/3 6/2
Novak Djokovic [2]	6/4 6/1 7/6(2)

Quarter-Finals

Andy Murray [1]	7/6(1) 6/4 6/4
Sam Querrey [24]	5/7 7/6(5) 6/3 6/7(11) 6/3
Gilles Muller [16]	6/3 6/4 3/6 4/6 15/13
Marin Cilic [7]	6/2 6/2 6/2
Milos Raonic [6]	4/6 7/5 4/6 7/5 6/1
Roger Federer [3]	6/4 6/2 6/4
Tomas Berdych [11]	6/3 6/7(1) 6/3 3/6 6/3
Novak Djokovic [2]	6/2 7/6(5) 6/4

Semi-Finals

Sam Querrey [24]	3/6 6/4 6/7(4) 6/1 6/1
Marin Cilic [7]	3/6 7/6(6) 7/5 5/7 6/1
Roger Federer [3]	6/4 6/2 7/6(4)
Tomas Berdych [11]	7/6(2) 2/0 Ret'd

Final

Marin Cilic [7]	6/7(6) 6/4 7/6(3) 7/5
Roger Federer [3]	7/6(4) 7/6(4) 6/4

Champion

Roger Federer [3] 6/3 6/1 6/4

Heavy type denotes seeded players. The figure in brackets against names denotes the order in which they have been seeded. The figure in italics denotes ATP World Tour Ranking – 03.07.2017.
(WC)=Wild card. (Q)=Qualifier. (LL)=Lucky loser.

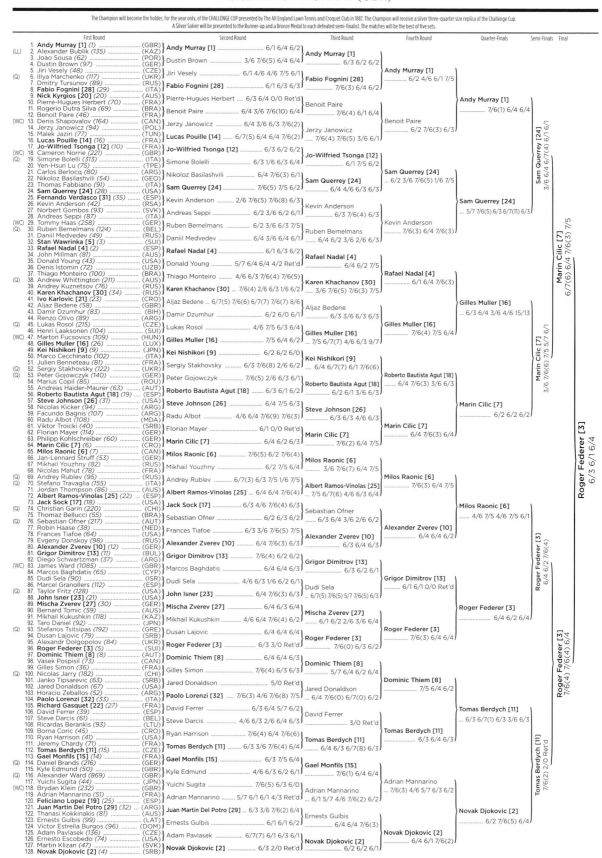

EVENT 2 – THE GENTLEMEN'S DOUBLES CHAMPIONSHIP 2017
Holders: PIERRE-HUGUES HERBERT (FRA) & NICOLAS MAHUT (FRA)

The Champions will become the holders, for the year only, of the CHALLENGE CUPS presented by the OXFORD UNIVERSITY LAWN TENNIS CLUB in 1884 and the late SIR HERBERT WILBERFORCE in 1937.
The Champions will receive a silver three-quarter size replica of the Challenge Cup. A Silver Salver will be presented to each of the Runners-up, and a Bronze Medal to each defeated semi-finalist. The matches will be the best of five sets.

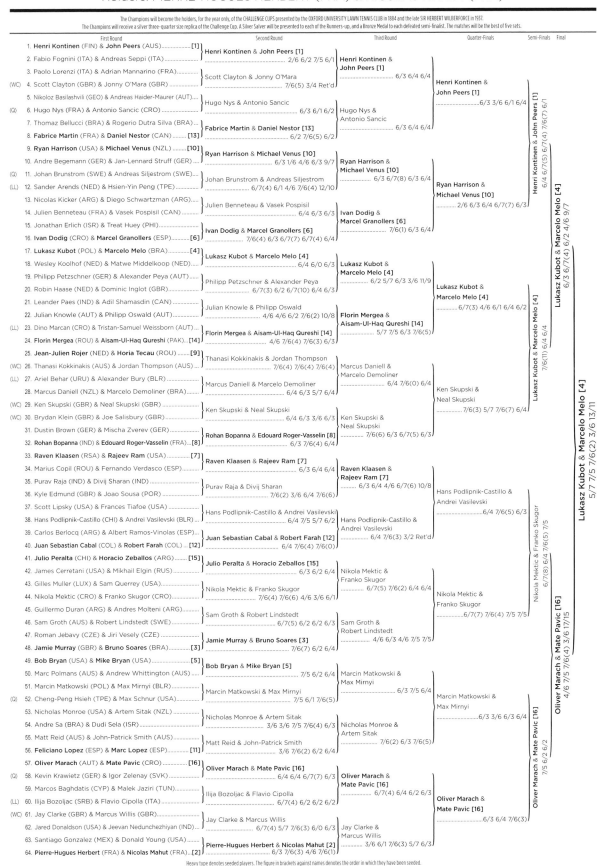

	First Round	Second Round	Third Round	Quarter-Finals	Semi-Finals	Final

1. Henri Kontinen (FIN) & John Peers (AUS) [1]
2. Fabio Fognini (ITA) & Andreas Seppi (ITA)
  - Henri Kontinen & John Peers [1] — 2/6 6/2 7/5 6/1
3. Paolo Lorenzi (ITA) & Adrian Mannarino (FRA)
(WC) 4. Scott Clayton (GBR) & Jonny O'Mara (GBR)
  - Scott Clayton & Jonny O'Mara — 7/6(5) 3/4 Ret'd
  - Henri Kontinen & John Peers [1] — 6/3 6/4 6/4
5. Nikoloz Basilashvili (GEO) & Andreas Haider-Maurer (AUT)
(Q) 6. Hugo Nys (FRA) & Antonio Sancic (CRO)
  - Hugo Nys & Antonio Sancic — 6/3 6/1 6/2
7. Thomaz Bellucci (BRA) & Rogerio Dutra Silva (BRA)
8. Fabrice Martin (FRA) & Daniel Nestor (CAN) [13]
  - Fabrice Martin & Daniel Nestor [13] — 6/2 7/6(5) 6/2
  - Hugo Nys & Antonio Sancic — 6/3 6/4 6/4
  - Henri Kontinen & John Peers [1] — 6/3 3/6 6/1 6/4

9. Ryan Harrison (USA) & Michael Venus (NZL) [10]
10. Andre Begemann (GER) & Jan-Lennard Struff (GER)
  - Ryan Harrison & Michael Venus [10] — 6/3 1/6 4/6 6/3 9/7
(Q) 11. Johan Brunstrom (SWE) & Andreas Siljestrom (SWE)
(LL) 12. Sander Arends (NED) & Hsien-Yin Peng (TPE)
  - Johan Brunstrom & Andreas Siljestrom — 6/7(4) 6/1 4/6 7/6(4) 12/10
  - Ryan Harrison & Michael Venus [10] — 6/3 6/7(8) 6/3 6/4
13. Nicolas Kicker (ARG) & Diego Schwartzman (ARG)
14. Julien Benneteau (FRA) & Vasek Pospisil (CAN)
  - Julien Benneteau & Vasek Pospisil — 6/4 6/3 6/3
15. Jonathan Erlich (ISR) & Treat Huey (PHI)
16. Ivan Dodig (CRO) & Marcel Granollers (ESP) [6]
  - Ivan Dodig & Marcel Granollers [6] — 7/6(4) 6/3 6/7(7) 7/6(4) 6/4
  - Ivan Dodig & Marcel Granollers [6] — 7/6(1) 6/3 6/4
  - Ryan Harrison & Michael Venus [10] — 2/6 6/3 6/4 6/7(7) 6/3
  - Henri Kontinen & John Peers [1] — 6/4 6/7(5) 6/7(4) 7/6(7) 6/1

17. Lukasz Kubot (POL) & Marcelo Melo (BRA) [4]
18. Wesley Koolhof (NED) & Matwe Middelkoop (NED)
  - Lukasz Kubot & Marcelo Melo [4] — 6/4 6/0 6/3
19. Philipp Petzschner (GER) & Alexander Peya (AUT)
20. Robin Haase (NED) & Dominic Inglot (GBR)
  - Philipp Petzschner & Alexander Peya — 6/7(3) 6/2 6/7(10) 6/4 6/3
  - Lukasz Kubot & Marcelo Melo [4] — 6/2 5/7 6/3 3/6 11/9
21. Leander Paes (IND) & Adil Shamasdin (CAN)
22. Julian Knowle (AUT) & Philipp Oswald (AUT)
  - Julian Knowle & Philipp Oswald — 4/6 4/6 6/2 7/6(2) 10/8
  - Florin Mergea & Aisam-Ul-Haq Qureshi [14] — 5/7 7/5 6/3 7/6(5)
(LL) 23. Dino Marcan (CRO) & Tristan-Samuel Weissborn (AUT)
24. Florin Mergea (ROU) & Aisam-Ul-Haq Qureshi (PAK) [14]
  - Florin Mergea & Aisam-Ul-Haq Qureshi [14] — 4/6 7/6(4) 7/6(3) 6/3
  - Lukasz Kubot & Marcelo Melo [4] — 6/7(3) 4/6 6/1 6/4 6/2
  - Lukasz Kubot & Marcelo Melo [4] — 7/6(11) 6/4 6/4

25. Jean-Julien Rojer (NED) & Horia Tecau (ROU) [9]
(WC) 26. Thanasi Kokkinakis (AUS) & Jordan Thompson (AUS)
  - Thanasi Kokkinakis & Jordan Thompson — 7/6(1) 7/6(4) 7/6(4)
(LL) 27. Ariel Behar (URU) & Alexander Bury (BLR)
28. Marcus Daniell (NZL) & Marcelo Demoliner (BRA)
  - Marcus Daniell & Marcelo Demoliner — 6/4 6/3 5/7 6/4
  - Marcus Daniell & Marcelo Demoliner — 6/4 7/6(0) 6/4
(WC) 29. Ken Skupski (GBR) & Neal Skupski (GBR)
(WC) 30. Brydan Klein (GBR) & Joe Salisbury (GBR)
  - Ken Skupski & Neal Skupski — 6/4 6/3 3/6 6/3
  - Ken Skupski & Neal Skupski — 7/6(6) 6/3 6/7(5) 6/3
31. Dustin Brown (GER) & Mischa Zverev (GER)
32. Rohan Bopanna (IND) & Edouard Roger-Vasselin (FRA) [8]
  - Rohan Bopanna & Edouard Roger-Vasselin [8] — 6/3 7/6(4) 6/4
  - Ken Skupski & Neal Skupski — 7/6(3) 5/7 7/6(7) 6/4

33. Raven Klaasen (RSA) & Rajeev Ram (USA) [7]
34. Marius Copil (ROU) & Fernando Verdasco (ESP)
  - Raven Klaasen & Rajeev Ram [7] — 6/3 6/4 6/4
35. Purav Raja (IND) & Divij Sharan (IND)
36. Kyle Edmund (GBR) & Joao Sousa (POR)
  - Purav Raja & Divij Sharan — 7/6(2) 3/6 6/4 7/6(6)
  - Raven Klaasen & Rajeev Ram [7] — 6/3 6/4 4/6 6/7(5) 10/8
37. Scott Lipsky (USA) & Frances Tiafoe (USA)
38. Hans Podlipnik-Castillo (CHI) & Andrei Vasilevski (BLR)
  - Hans Podlipnik-Castillo & Andrei Vasilevski — 6/4 7/5 5/7 6/2
  - Hans Podlipnik-Castillo & Andrei Vasilevski — 6/4 7/6(3) 3/2 Ret'd
39. Carlos Berlocq (ARG) & Albert Ramos-Vinolas (ESP)
40. Juan Sebastian Cabal (COL) & Robert Farah (COL) [12]
  - Juan Sebastian Cabal & Robert Farah [12] — 6/4 6/7(5) 6/0
  - Hans Podlipnik-Castillo & Andrei Vasilevski — 6/4 7/6(5) 6/3

41. Julio Peralta (CHI) & Horacio Zeballos (ARG) [15]
42. James Cerretani (USA) & Mikhail Elgin (RUS)
  - Julio Peralta & Horacio Zeballos [15] — 6/3 6/2 6/4
43. Gilles Muller (LUX) & Sam Querrey (USA)
44. Nikola Mektic (CRO) & Franko Skugor (CRO)
  - Nikola Mektic & Franko Skugor — 7/6(4) 7/6(6) 4/6 3/6 6/1
  - Nikola Mektic & Franko Skugor — 6/7(5) 7/6(2) 6/4 6/4
  - Nikola Mektic & Franko Skugor — 6/7(8) 6/4 7/6(5) 7/5
45. Guillermo Duran (ARG) & Andres Molteni (ARG)
46. Sam Groth (AUS) & Robert Lindstedt (SWE)
  - Sam Groth & Robert Lindstedt — 6/7(5) 6/2 6/2 6/3
  - Sam Groth & Robert Lindstedt — 4/6 6/3 4/6 7/5 7/5
47. Roman Jebavy (CZE) & Jiri Vesely (CZE)
48. Jamie Murray (GBR) & Bruno Soares (BRA) [3]
  - Jamie Murray & Bruno Soares [3] — 7/6(7) 6/2 6/4

49. Bob Bryan (USA) & Mike Bryan (USA) [5]
50. Marc Polmans (AUS) & Andrew Whittington (AUS)
  - Bob Bryan & Mike Bryan [5] — 7/5 6/2 6/4
51. Marcin Matkowski (POL) & Max Mirnyi (BLR)
(Q) 52. Cheng-Peng Hsieh (TPE) & Max Schnur (USA)
  - Marcin Matkowski & Max Mirnyi — 7/5 6/1 7/6(5)
  - Marcin Matkowski & Max Mirnyi — 6/3 7/5 6/4
  - Marcin Matkowski & Max Mirnyi — 6/3 3/6 6/3 6/4
53. Nicholas Monroe (USA) & Artem Sitak (NZL)
54. Andre Sa (BRA) & Dudi Sela (ISR)
  - Nicholas Monroe & Artem Sitak — 3/6 3/6 7/5 7/6(4) 6/4
  - Nicholas Monroe & Artem Sitak — 7/6(2) 6/3 7/6(5)
55. Matt Reid (AUS) & John-Patrick Smith (AUS)
56. Feliciano Lopez (ESP) & Marc Lopez (ESP) [11]
  - Matt Reid & John-Patrick Smith — 3/6 7/6(2) 6/2 6/4

57. Oliver Marach (AUT) & Mate Pavic (CRO) [16]
(Q) 58. Kevin Krawietz (GER) & Igor Zelenay (SVK)
  - Oliver Marach & Mate Pavic [16] — 6/4 6/4 6/7(7) 6/3
59. Marcos Baghdatis (CYP) & Malek Jaziri (TUN)
(LL) 60. Ilija Bozoljac (SRB) & Flavio Cipolla (ITA)
  - Ilija Bozoljac & Flavio Cipolla — 6/7(4) 6/2 6/2 6/2
  - Oliver Marach & Mate Pavic [16] — 6/7(4) 6/4 6/2 6/3
  - Oliver Marach & Mate Pavic [16] — 6/3 6/4 7/6(3)
(WC) 61. Jay Clarke (GBR) & Marcus Willis (GBR)
62. Jared Donaldson (USA) & Jeevan Nedunchezhiyan (IND)
  - Jay Clarke & Marcus Willis — 6/7(4) 5/7 7/6(3) 6/0 6/3
  - Jay Clarke & Marcus Willis — 3/6 6/1 7/6(3) 5/7 6/3
63. Santiago Gonzalez (MEX) & Donald Young (USA)
64. Pierre-Hugues Herbert (FRA) & Nicolas Mahut (FRA) [2]
  - Pierre-Hugues Herbert & Nicolas Mahut [2] — 6/3 7/6(3) 4/6 6/1

Quarter-Finals / Semi-Finals / Final

Henri Kontinen & John Peers [1]

Lukasz Kubot & Marcelo Melo [4] — 6/3 6/7(4) 6/2 4/6 9/7

Lukasz Kubot & Marcelo Melo [4] — 5/7 7/5 7/6(2) 3/6 13/11

Ken Skupski & Neal Skupski — 7/6(3) 5/7 7/6(7) 6/4

Hans Podlipnik-Castillo & Andrei Vasilevski — 6/4 7/6(5) 6/3

Nikola Mektic & Franko Skugor — 6/7(8) 6/4 7/6(5) 7/5

Oliver Marach & Mate Pavic [16] — 4/6 7/5 7/6(4) 3/6 17/15

Oliver Marach & Mate Pavic [16] — 7/5 6/2 6/2

Lukasz Kubot & Marcelo Melo [4] — 5/7 7/5 7/6(2) 3/6 13/11

Heavy type denotes seeded players. The figure in brackets against names denotes the order in which they have been seeded.
(WC)=Wild cards. (Q)=Qualifiers. (LL)=Lucky losers.

EVENT 3 – THE LADIES' SINGLES CHAMPIONSHIP 2017
Holder: SERENA WILLIAMS (USA)

The Champion will become the holder, for the year only, of the CHALLENGE TROPHY presented by The All England Lawn Tennis and Croquet Club in 1886. The Champion will receive a silver three-quarter size replica of the Challenge Trophy.
A Silver Salver will be presented to the Runner-up and a Bronze Medal to each defeated semi-finalist. The matches will be the best of three sets.

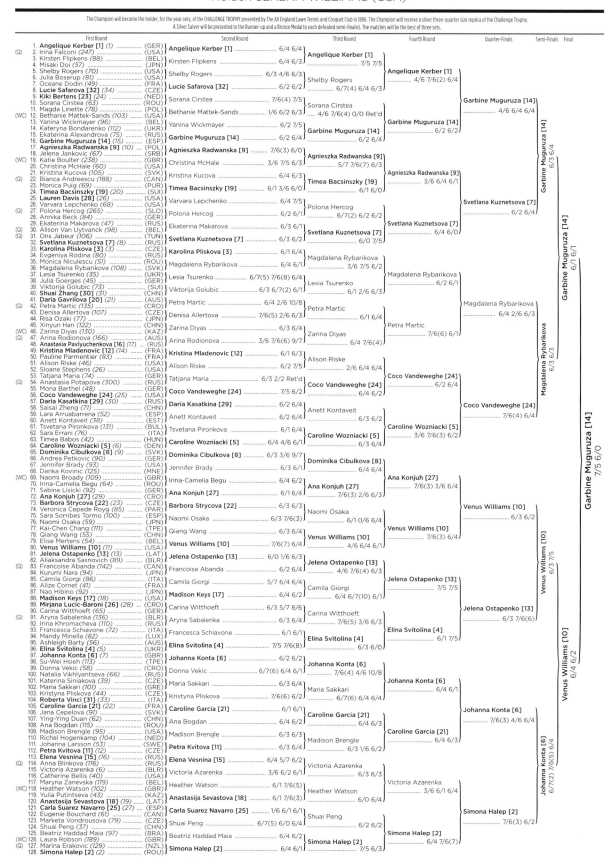

Heavy type denotes seeded players. The figure in brackets against names denotes the order in which they have been seeded. The figure in italics denotes WTA Ranking – 03.07.2017.
(WC)=Wild card. (Q)=Qualifier. (LL)=Lucky loser.

EVENT 4 – THE LADIES' DOUBLES CHAMPIONSHIP 2017
Holders: SERENA WILLIAMS (USA) & VENUS WILLIAMS (USA)

The Champions will become the holders, for the year only, of the CHALLENGE CUPS presented by H.R.H. PRINCESS MARINA, DUCHESS OF KENT, the late President of The All England Lawn Tennis and Croquet Club in 1949 and The All England Lawn Tennis and Croquet Club in 2001.
The Champions will receive a silver three-quarter size replica of the Challenge Cup. A Silver Salver will be presented to each of the Runners-up and a Bronze Medal to each defeated semi-finalist. The matches are the best of three sets.

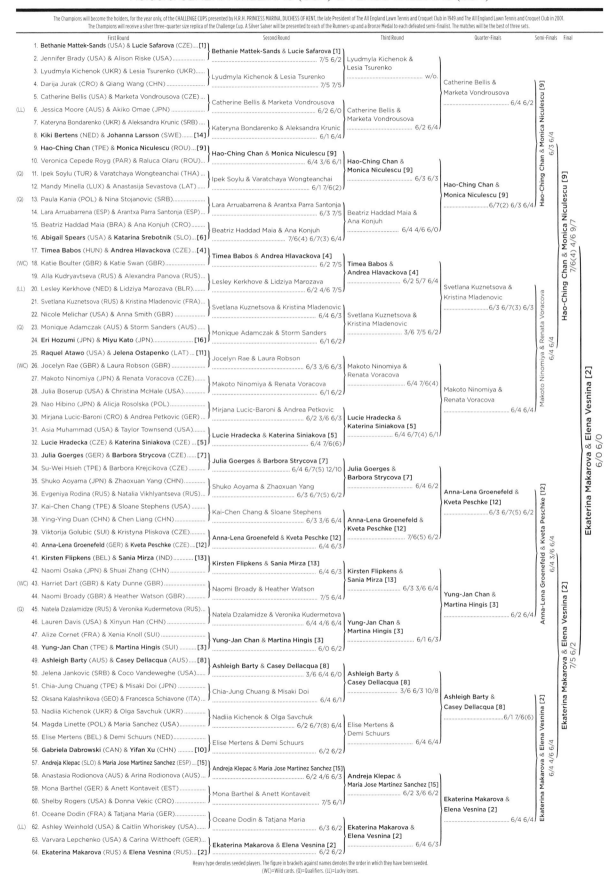

First Round — Second Round — Third Round — Quarter-Finals — Semi-Finals — Final

1. **Bethanie Mattek-Sands** (USA) & **Lucie Safarova** (CZE)....**[1]**
2. Jennifer Brady (USA) & Alison Riske (USA)
   — Bethanie Mattek-Sands & Lucie Safarova [1] — 7/5 6/2
3. Lyudmyla Kichenok (UKR) & Lesia Tsurenko (UKR)
4. Darija Jurak (CRO) & Qiang Wang (CHN)
   — Lyudmyla Kichenok & Lesia Tsurenko — 7/5 7/5
   — Lyudmyla Kichenok & Lesia Tsurenko — w/o.
5. Catherine Bellis (USA) & Marketa Vondrousova (CZE)
(LL) 6. Jessica Moore (AUS) & Akiko Omae (JPN)
   — Catherine Bellis & Marketa Vondrousova — 6/2 6/0
7. Kateryna Bondarenko (UKR) & Aleksandra Krunic (SRB)
8. **Kiki Bertens** (NED) & **Johanna Larsson** (SWE)....**[14]**
   — Kateryna Bondarenko & Aleksandra Krunic — 6/1 6/4
   — Catherine Bellis & Marketa Vondrousova — 6/2 6/4
   — Catherine Bellis & Marketa Vondrousova — 6/4 6/2

9. **Hao-Ching Chan** (TPE) & **Monica Niculescu** (ROU)....**[9]**
10. Veronica Cepede Royg (PAR) & Raluca Olaru (ROU)
    — Hao-Ching Chan & Monica Niculescu [9] — 6/4 3/6 6/1
(Q) 11. Ipek Soylu (TUR) & Varatchaya Wongteanchai (THA)
12. Mandy Minella (LUX) & Anastasija Sevastova (LAT)
    — Ipek Soylu & Varatchaya Wongteanchai — 6/1 7/6(2)
    — Hao-Ching Chan & Monica Niculescu [9] — 6/3 6/3
(Q) 13. Paula Kania (POL) & Nina Stojanovic (SRB)
14. Lara Arruabarrena (ESP) & Arantxa Parra Santonja (ESP)
    — Lara Arruabarrena & Arantxa Parra Santonja — 6/3 7/5
15. Beatriz Haddad Maia (BRA) & Ana Konjuh (CRO)
16. **Abigail Spears** (USA) & **Katarina Srebotnik** (SLO)....**[6]**
    — Beatriz Haddad Maia & Ana Konjuh — 7/6(4) 6/7(3) 6/4
    — Beatriz Haddad Maia & Ana Konjuh — 6/4 4/6 6/0
    — Hao-Ching Chan & Monica Niculescu [9] — 6/7(2) 6/3 6/4

17. **Timea Babos** (HUN) & **Andrea Hlavackova** (CZE)....**[4]**
(WC) 18. Katie Boulter (GBR) & Katie Swan (GBR)
    — Timea Babos & Andrea Hlavackova [4] — 6/2 7/5
19. Alla Kudryavtseva (RUS) & Alexandra Panova (RUS)
(LL) 20. Lesley Kerkhove (NED) & Lidziya Marozava (BLR)
    — Lesley Kerkhove & Lidziya Marozava — 6/2 4/6 7/5
    — Timea Babos & Andrea Hlavackova [4] — 6/2 5/7 6/4
21. Svetlana Kuznetsova (RUS) & Kristina Mladenovic (FRA)
22. Nicole Melichar (USA) & Anna Smith (GBR)
    — Svetlana Kuznetsova & Kristina Mladenovic — 6/4 6/3
(Q) 23. Monique Adamczak (AUS) & Storm Sanders (AUS)
24. **Eri Hozumi** (JPN) & **Miyu Kato** (JPN)....**[16]**
    — Monique Adamczak & Storm Sanders — 6/1 6/2
    — Svetlana Kuznetsova & Kristina Mladenovic — 3/6 7/5 6/2
    — Svetlana Kuznetsova & Kristina Mladenovic — 6/3 6/7(3) 6/3

25. **Raquel Atawo** (USA) & **Jelena Ostapenko** (LAT)....**[11]**
(WC) 26. Jocelyn Rae (GBR) & Laura Robson (GBR)
    — Jocelyn Rae & Laura Robson — 6/3 3/6 6/3
27. Makoto Ninomiya (JPN) & Renata Voracova (CZE)
28. Julia Boserup (USA) & Christina McHale (USA)
    — Makoto Ninomiya & Renata Voracova — 6/1 6/2
    — Makoto Ninomiya & Renata Voracova — 6/4 7/6(4)
29. Nao Hibino (JPN) & Alicja Rosolska (POL)
30. Mirjana Lucic-Baroni (CRO) & Andrea Petkovic (GER)
    — Mirjana Lucic-Baroni & Andrea Petkovic — 6/2 3/6 6/3
31. Asia Muhammad (USA) & Taylor Townsend (USA)
32. **Lucie Hradecka** (CZE) & **Katerina Siniakova** (CZE)....**[5]**
    — Lucie Hradecka & Katerina Siniakova [5] — 6/4 7/6(6)
    — Lucie Hradecka & Katerina Siniakova [5] — 6/4 6/7(4) 6/1
    — Makoto Ninomiya & Renata Voracova — 6/4 6/4

33. **Julia Goerges** (GER) & **Barbora Strycova** (CZE)....**[7]**
34. Su-Wei Hsieh (TPE) & Barbora Krejcikova (CZE)
    — Julia Goerges & Barbora Strycova [7] — 6/4 6/7(5) 12/10
35. Shuko Aoyama (JPN) & Zhaoxuan Yang (CHN)
36. Evgeniya Rodina (RUS) & Natalia Vikhlyantseva (RUS)
    — Shuko Aoyama & Zhaoxuan Yang — 6/3 6/7(5) 6/2
    — Julia Goerges & Barbora Strycova [7] — 6/4 6/2
37. Kai-Chen Chang (TPE) & Sloane Stephens (USA)
38. Ying-Ying Duan (CHN) & Chen Liang (CHN)
    — Kai-Chen Chang & Sloane Stephens — 6/3 3/6 6/4
39. Viktorija Golubic (SUI) & Kristyna Pliskova (CZE)
40. **Anna-Lena Groenefeld** (GER) & **Kveta Peschke** (CZE)....**[12]**
    — Anna-Lena Groenefeld & Kveta Peschke [12] — 6/4 6/3
    — Anna-Lena Groenefeld & Kveta Peschke [12] — 7/6(5) 6/2
    — Anna-Lena Groenefeld & Kveta Peschke [12] — 6/3 6/7(5) 6/2

41. **Kirsten Flipkens** (BEL) & **Sania Mirza** (IND)....**[13]**
42. Naomi Osaka (JPN) & Shuai Zhang (CHN)
    — Kirsten Flipkens & Sania Mirza [13] — 6/4 6/3
(WC) 43. Harriet Dart (GBR) & Katy Dunne (GBR)
44. Naomi Broady (GBR) & Heather Watson (GBR)
    — Naomi Broady & Heather Watson — 7/5 6/4
    — Kirsten Flipkens & Sania Mirza [13] — 6/3 3/6 6/4
(Q) 45. Natela Dzalamidze (RUS) & Veronika Kudermetova (RUS)
46. Lauren Davis (USA) & Xinyun Han (CHN)
    — Natela Dzalamidze & Veronika Kudermetova — 6/4 4/6 6/4
47. Alize Cornet (FRA) & Xenia Knoll (SUI)
48. **Yung-Jan Chan** (TPE) & **Martina Hingis** (SUI)....**[3]**
    — Yung-Jan Chan & Martina Hingis [3] — 6/0 6/2
    — Yung-Jan Chan & Martina Hingis [3] — 6/1 6/3
    — Yung-Jan Chan & Martina Hingis [3] — 6/2 6/4

49. **Ashleigh Barty** (AUS) & **Casey Dellacqua** (AUS)....**[8]**
50. Jelena Jankovic (SRB) & Coco Vandeweghe (USA)
    — Ashleigh Barty & Casey Dellacqua [8] — 3/6 6/4 6/0
51. Chia-Jung Chuang (TPE) & Misaki Doi (JPN)
52. Oksana Kalashnikova (GEO) & Francesca Schiavone (ITA)
    — Chia-Jung Chuang & Misaki Doi — 6/4 6/1
    — Ashleigh Barty & Casey Dellacqua [8] — 3/6 6/3 10/8
53. Nadiia Kichenok (UKR) & Olga Savchuk (UKR)
54. Magda Linette (POL) & Maria Sanchez (USA)
    — Nadiia Kichenok & Olga Savchuk — 6/2 6/7(8) 6/4
55. Elise Mertens (BEL) & Demi Schuurs (NED)
56. **Gabriela Dabrowski** (CAN) & **Yifan Xu** (CHN)....**[10]**
    — Elise Mertens & Demi Schuurs — 6/2 6/2
    — Elise Mertens & Demi Schuurs — 6/4 6/4
    — Ashleigh Barty & Casey Dellacqua [8] — 6/1 7/6(6)

57. **Andreja Klepac** (SLO) & **Maria Jose Martinez Sanchez** (ESP)....**[15]**
58. Anastasia Rodionova (AUS) & Arina Rodionova (AUS)
    — Andreja Klepac & Maria Jose Martinez Sanchez [15] — 6/2 4/6 6/3
59. Mona Barthel (GER) & Anett Kontaveit (EST)
60. Shelby Rogers (USA) & Donna Vekic (CRO)
    — Mona Barthel & Anett Kontaveit — 7/5 6/1
    — Andreja Klepac & Maria Jose Martinez Sanchez [15] — 6/2 3/6 6/2
61. Oceane Dodin (FRA) & Tatjana Maria (GER)
(LL) 62. Ashley Weinhold (USA) & Caitlin Whoriskey (USA)
    — Oceane Dodin & Tatjana Maria — 6/3 6/2
63. Varvara Lepchenko (USA) & Carina Witthoeft (GER)
64. **Ekaterina Makarova** (RUS) & **Elena Vesnina** (RUS)....**[2]**
    — Ekaterina Makarova & Elena Vesnina [2] — 6/2 6/2
    — Ekaterina Makarova & Elena Vesnina [2] — 6/4 6/3
    — Ekaterina Makarova & Elena Vesnina [2] — 6/4 6/4

Catherine Bellis & Marketa Vondrousova — 6/4 6/2

Hao-Ching Chan & Monica Niculescu [9] — 6/3 6/4

Svetlana Kuznetsova & Kristina Mladenovic — 6/4 6/4

Makoto Ninomiya & Renata Voracova — 4/6 3/6 6/4

Hao-Ching Chan & Monica Niculescu [9] — 7/6(4) 4/6 9/7

Anna-Lena Groenefeld & Kveta Peschke [12] — 6/4 3/6 6/4

Yung-Jan Chan & Martina Hingis [3] — 6/2 6/4

Ashleigh Barty & Casey Dellacqua [8] — 6/4 4/6 6/4

Ekaterina Makarova & Elena Vesnina [2] — 4/6 6/4 6/4

Ekaterina Makarova & Elena Vesnina [2] — 7/5 6/2

Hao-Ching Chan & Monica Niculescu [9] — 6/3 6/4

Ekaterina Makarova & Elena Vesnina [2] — 6/0 6/0

Ekaterina Makarova & Elena Vesnina [2] — 6/0 6/0

Heavy type denotes seeded players. The figure in brackets against names denotes the order in which they have been seeded.
(WC)=Wild cards. (Q)=Qualifiers. (LL)=Lucky losers.

EVENT 5 – THE MIXED DOUBLES CHAMPIONSHIP 2017
Holders: HENRI KONTINEN (FIN) & HEATHER WATSON (GBR)

The Champions will become the holders, for the year only, of the CHALLENGE CUPS presented by members of the family of the late Mr. S. H. SMITH in 1949 and The All England Lawn Tennis and Croquet Club in 2001.
The Champions will receive a silver three-quarter size replica of the Challenge Cup. A Silver Salver will be presented to each of the Runners-up and a Bronze Medal to each defeated semi-finalist. The matches will be the best of three sets.

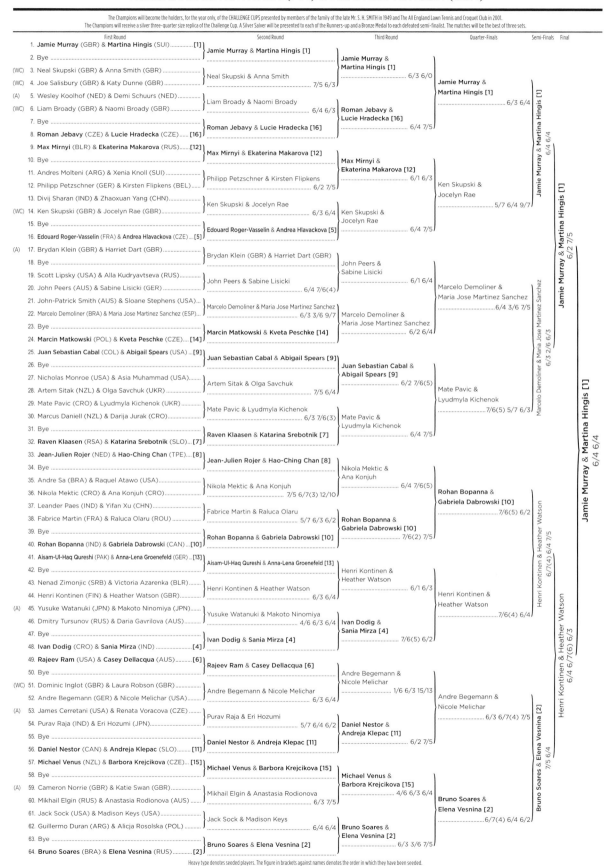

Heavy type denotes seeded players. The figure in brackets against names denotes the order in which they have been seeded.
(A)=Alternates. (WC)=Wild cards.

EVENT 6 – THE BOYS' SINGLES CHAMPIONSHIP 2017

Holder: DENIS SHAPOVALOV (CAN)

The Champion will become the holder, for the year only, of a Cup presented by The All England Lawn Tennis and Croquet Club.
The Champion will receive a three-quarter size Cup and the Runner-up will receive a Silver Salver. The matches will be the best of three sets.

First Round

(WC) 1. **Corentin Moutet [1]** *(20)* (FRA)
2. Sebastian Baez *(17)* (ARG)
3. Alafia Ayeni *(39)* (USA)
4. Menelaos Efstathiou *(49)* (CYP)
5. Tomas Machac *(40)* (CZE)
(WC) 6. Hamish Stewart *(196)* (GBR)
(Q) 7. Francesco Forti *(71)* (ITA)
8. **Thiago Seyboth Wild [13]** *(15)* (BRA)
9. **Jurij Rodionov [11]** *(11)* (AUT)
10. Louis Dussin *(86)* (FRA)
11. Chun Hsin Tseng *(41)* (TPE)
12. Shinji Hazawa *(52)* (JPN)
13. Artem Dubrivnyy *(42)* (RUS)
14. Alan Fernando Rubio Fierros *(44)* (MEX)
15. Blake Ellis *(34)* (AUS)
16. **Trent Bryde [7]** *(8)* (USA)
17. **Zsombor Piros [3]** *(4)* (HUN)
18. Timofey Skatov *(27)* (RUS)
(WC) 19. Max Stewart *(94)* (GBR)
20. Naoki Tajima *(45)* (JPN)
21. Axel Geller *(25)* (ARG)
22. Uisung Park *(47)* (KOR)
23. Danny Thomas *(22)* (USA)
24. **Zizou Bergs [14]** *(16)* (BEL)
25. **Yshai Oliel [12]** *(12)* (ISR)
26. Alexandre Rotsaert *(36)* (USA)
(Q) 27. Siddhant Banthia *(58)* (IND)
28. Matteo Martineau *(33)* (FRA)
(WC) 29. Aidan McHugh *(108)* (GBR)
30. Gianni Ross *(32)* (USA)
31. Ondrej Styler *(37)* (CZE)
32. **Marko Miladinovic [6]** *(7)* (SRB)
33. **Yuta Shimizu [5]** *(6)* (JPN)
34. Ryan Nijboer *(54)* (NED)
35. Patrick Kypson *(43)* (USA)
36. Alexey Zakharov *(38)* (RUS)
(Q) 37. Juan Alejandro Hernandez Serrano *(111)* (MEX)
(WC) 38. George Loffhagen *(172)* (GBR)
39. Emil Ruusuvuori *(26)* (FIN)
40. **Rudolf Molleker [9]** *(24)* (GER)
41. **Duarte Vale [15]** *(18)* (POR)
42. Michael Vrbensky *(21)* (CZE)
43. Sebastian Korda *(29)* (USA)
(Q) 44. James Kent Trotter *(115)* (JPN)
45. Constantin Bittoun Kouzmine *(23)* (FRA)
(WC) 46. Anton Matusevich *(120)* (GBR)
47. Sam Riffice *(46)* (USA)
48. **Yu Hsiou Hsu [4]** *(5)* (TPE)
49. **Alejandro Davidovich Fokina [8]** *(9)* (ESP)
50. Nicolas Mejia *(51)* (COL)
(Q) 51. Lukas Greif *(75)* (USA)
52. Dan Added *(35)* (FRA)
(Q) 53. Thomas Bosancic *(87)* (AUS)
(WC) 54. Barnaby Smith *(63)* (GBR)
55. Toru Horie *(48)* (JPN)
56. **Oliver Crawford [10]** *(10)* (USA)
57. **Juan Pablo Grassi Mazzuchi [16]** *(19)* (ARG)
58. Hugo Gaston *(57)* (FRA)
(Q) 59. Mattia Frinzi *(80)* (ITA)
60. Mohamed Ali Bellalouna *(73)* (TUN)
61. Vasil Kirkov *(30)* (USA)
(Q) 62. Joao Lucas Reis Da Silva *(98)* (BRA)
(WC) 63. Jack Draper *(122)* (GBR)
64. **Yibing Wu [2]** *(3)* (CHN)

Second Round

- **Corentin Moutet [1]** 6/4 6/3
- Menelaos Efstathiou 3/6 6/4 6/4
- Hamish Stewart 4/6 7/5 6/1
- Francesco Forti 6/4 6/4
- **Jurij Rodionov [11]** 7/6(5) 6/3
- Shinji Hazawa 3/6 7/6(10) 6/4
- Alan Fernando Rubio Fierros 6/2 5/7 6/4
- Blake Ellis 7/6(2) 6/7(5) 6/1
- Timofey Skatov 6/2 6/4
- Naoki Tajima 6/4 6/4
- Axel Geller 6/3 6/3
- Danny Thomas 6/4 6/4
- **Yshai Oliel [12]** 6/3 6/2
- Matteo Martineau 3/6 6/2 7/5
- Aidan McHugh 6/2 2/6 6/4
- **Marko Miladinovic [6]** 6/3 7/6(7)
- **Yuta Shimizu [5]** 6/1 7/6(6)
- Patrick Kypson 6/4 7/6(6)
- George Loffhagen 6/3 4/6 6/2
- **Rudolf Molleker [9]** 6/3 3/1 Ret'd
- Michael Vrbensky 6/4 7/6(6)
- Sebastian Korda 3/6 7/5 6/4
- Constantin Bittoun Kouzmine 6/3 3/0 Ret'd
- Sam Riffice 6/4 7/5
- **Alejandro Davidovich Fokina [8]** 6/4 6/4
- Dan Added 5/7 7/5 6/2
- Barnaby Smith 5/7 6/4 6/3
- **Oliver Crawford [10]** 6/4 7/5
- **Juan Pablo Grassi Mazzuchi [16]** 6/2 7/6(5)
- Mohamed Ali Bellalouna 6/4 6/4
- Vasil Kirkov 2/6 7/5 7/5
- **Yibing Wu [2]** 6/3 6/2

Third Round

- **Corentin Moutet [1]** 6/3 6/2
- Francesco Forti 7/5 7/5
- **Jurij Rodionov [11]** 7/5 7/5
- Blake Ellis 6/3 7/6(3)
- Naoki Tajima 7/6(9) 6/3
- Axel Geller 6/1 6/0
- Matteo Martineau 6/4 6/4
- Aidan McHugh 6/0 7/6(4)
- Patrick Kypson 7/5 4/6 7/5
- George Loffhagen 6/4 6/4
- Michael Vrbensky 6/0 7/6(5)
- Constantin Bittoun Kouzmine 7/6(8) 7/6(5)
- Alejandro Davidovich Fokina [8] 6/3 6/1
- **Oliver Crawford [10]** 7/6(3) 6/2
- Mohamed Ali Bellalouna 7/6(5) 6/3
- **Yibing Wu [2]** 6/1 6/1

Quarter-Finals

- **Corentin Moutet [1]** 7/5 6/1
- **Jurij Rodionov [11]** 6/3 6/7(4) 6/3
- Axel Geller 6/3 3/6 6/1
- Matteo Martineau 6/3 6/7(12) 6/2
- Patrick Kypson 4/6 6/0 8/6
- Michael Vrbensky 6/4 6/4
- Alejandro Davidovich Fokina [8] 6/1 6/3
- **Yibing Wu [2]** 6/2 6/2

Semi-Finals

- **Corentin Moutet [1]** 6/2 6/4
- Axel Geller 6/3 7/5
- Patrick Kypson 6/2 6/1
- Alejandro Davidovich Fokina [8] 6/2 6/4

Final

- Axel Geller 1/6 6/3 6/3
- Alejandro Davidovich Fokina [8] 6/4 6/4

Alejandro Davidovich Fokina [8] 7/6(2) 6/3

Heavy type denotes seeded players. The figure in brackets against names denotes the order in which they have been seeded. The Committee reserves the right to alter the seeding order in the event of withdrawals.
(WC)=Wild card. (Q)=Qualifier. (LL)=Lucky loser.

EVENT 7 – THE BOYS' DOUBLES CHAMPIONSHIP 2017

Holders: KENNETH RAISMA (EST) & STEFANOS TSITSIPAS (GRE)

The Champions will become the holders, for the year only, of a Cup presented by The All England Lawn Tennis and Croquet Club.
The Champions will receive a three-quarter size Cup and the Runners-up will receive Silver Salvers. The matches will be the best of three sets.

First Round

1. **Zsombor Piros** (HUN) & **Yibing Wu** (CHN) [1]
2. Mohamed Ali Bellalouna (TUN) & Joao Lucas Reis Da Silva (BRA)
3. Sebastian Korda (USA) & Nicolas Mejia (COL)
(WC) 4. Jack Molloy (GBR) & Barnaby Smith (GBR)
5. Toru Horie (JPN) & Yuta Shimizu (JPN)
6. Oliver Crawford (USA) & Patrick Kypson (USA)
7. Louis Dussin (FRA) & Hugo Gaston (FRA)
8. **Gianni Ross** (USA) & **Thiago Seyboth Wild** (BRA) [5]
9. **Jurij Rodionov** (AUT) & **Michael Vrbensky** (CZE) [3]
(WC) 10. Jack Draper (GBR) & George Loffhagen (GBR)
11. Vasil Kirkov (USA) & Danny Thomas (USA)
12. Sam Riffice (USA) & Duarte Vale (POR)
13. Juan Alejandro Hernandez Serrano (MEX) & Alan Fernando Rubio Fierros (MEX)
14. Simon Carr (IRL) & Alexandre Rotsaert (USA)
15. Ondrej Styler (CZE) & Alexey Zakharov (RUS)
16. **Marko Miladinovic** (SRB) & **Chun Hsin Tseng** (TPE) [7]
17. **Sebastian Baez** (ARG) & **Juan Pablo Grassi Mazzuchi** (ARG) [8]
(WC) 18. Finn Bass (GBR) & Aidan McHugh (GBR)
19. Andrew Fenty (USA) & Yshai Oliel (ISR)
(A) 20. Brian Cernoch (USA) & Jesper De Jong (NED)
21. Thomas Bosancic (AUS) & Lukas Greif (USA)
22. Constantin Bittoun Kouzmine (FRA) & Uisung Park (KOR)
23. Blake Ellis (AUS) & Matteo Martineau (FRA)
24. **Dan Added** (FRA) & **Zizou Bergs** (BEL) [9]
25. **Alafia Ayeni** (USA) & **Trent Bryde** (USA) [6]
(A) 26. Hamish Stewart (GBR) & Dominic West (GBR)
27. Tomas Machac (CZE) & Timofey Skatov (RUS)
28. Menelaos Efstathiou (CYP) & Ryan Nijboer (NED)
29. Shinji Hazawa (JPN) & Naoki Tajima (JPN)
30. Francesco Forti (ITA) & Mattia Frinzi (ITA)
31. Siddhant Banthia (IND) & James Kent Trotter (JPN)
32. **Axel Geller** (ARG) & **Yu Hsiou Hsu** (TPE) [2]

Second Round

- **Zsombor Piros & Yibing Wu [1]** 6/1 6/4
- Sebastian Korda & Nicolas Mejia 6/3 6/4
- Toru Horie & Yuta Shimizu 6/3 6/2
- Louis Dussin & Hugo Gaston 7/6(5) 7/6(6)
- **Jurij Rodionov & Michael Vrbensky [3]** 7/6(7) 6/3
- Vasil Kirkov & Danny Thomas 6/4 6/4
- Simon Carr & Alexandre Rotsaert 5/7 6/1 6/4
- Ondrej Styler & Alexey Zakharov 6/2 4/6 7/5
- Finn Bass & Aidan McHugh 6/3 6/1
- Andrew Fenty & Yshai Oliel 6/4 6/2
- Constantin Bittoun Kouzmine & Uisung Park w/o.
- Blake Ellis & Matteo Martineau 6/3 7/6(5)
- **Alafia Ayeni & Trent Bryde [6]** 6/3 6/4
- Menelaos Efstathiou & Ryan Nijboer 6/4 3/6 6/3
- Francesco Forti & Mattia Frinzi 3/6 6/1 8/6
- **Axel Geller & Yu Hsiou Hsu [2]** 4/6 6/3 9/7

Quarter-Finals

- Sebastian Korda & Nicolas Mejia 7/6(2) 4/6 6/4
- Toru Horie & Yuta Shimizu 7/6(3) 7/6(4)
- **Jurij Rodionov & Michael Vrbensky [3]** 3/6 7/5 6/3
- Ondrej Styler & Alexey Zakharov 6/2 6/2
- Andrew Fenty & Yshai Oliel 7/6(3) 6/4
- Blake Ellis & Matteo Martineau 6/3 6/2
- Menelaos Efstathiou & Ryan Nijboer 6/4 1/6 6/4
- **Axel Geller & Yu Hsiou Hsu [2]** 6/3 6/2

Semi-Finals

- Sebastian Korda & Nicolas Mejia 1/6 6/3 6/2
- **Jurij Rodionov & Michael Vrbensky [3]** 7/6(7) 7/6(5)
- Blake Ellis & Matteo Martineau 6/3 6/2
- **Axel Geller & Yu Hsiou Hsu [2]** 6/2 6/1

Final

- Jurij Rodionov & Michael Vrbensky [3] 6/3 6/4
- Axel Geller & Yu Hsiou Hsu [2] 7/6(5) 6/7(3) 10/8

Axel Geller & Yu Hsiou Hsu [2] 6/4 6/4

Heavy type denotes seeded players. The figure in brackets against names denotes the order in which they have been seeded. The Committee reserves the right to alter the seeding order in the event of withdrawals.
(WC)=Wild cards. (A)=Alternates.

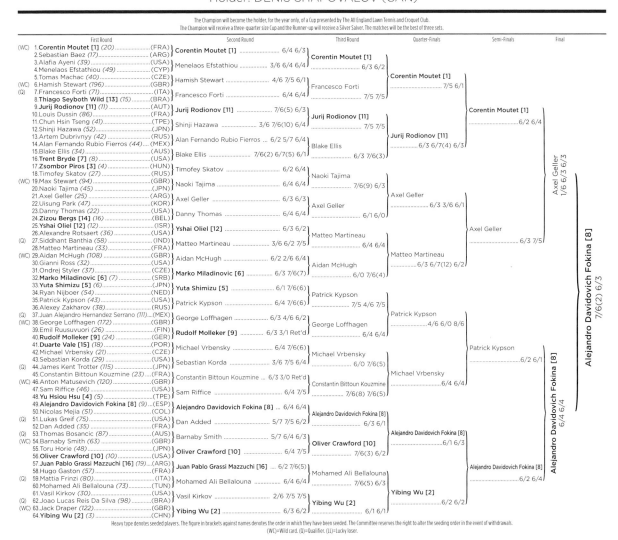

EVENT 8 – THE GIRLS' SINGLES CHAMPIONSHIP 2017
Holder: ANASTASIA POTAPOVA (RUS)

The Champion will become the holder, for the year only, of a Cup presented by The All England Lawn Tennis and Croquet Club.
The Champion will receive a three-quarter size Cup and the Runner-up will receive a Silver Salver. The matches will be the best of three sets.

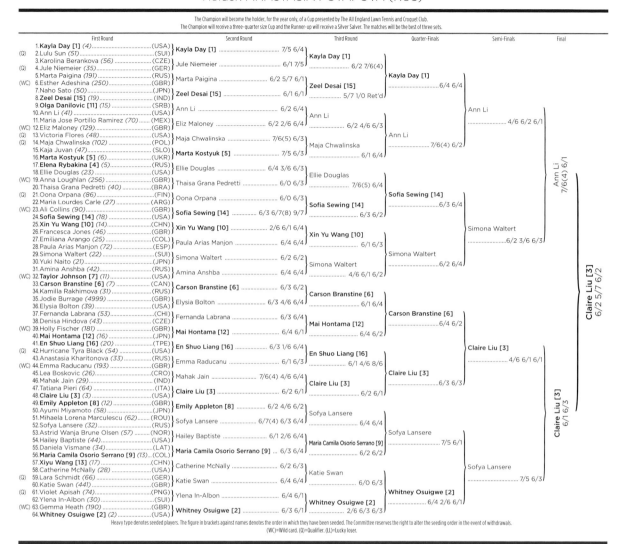

Heavy type denotes seeded players. The figure in brackets against names denotes the order in which they have been seeded. The Committee reserves the right to alter the seeding order in the event of withdrawals.
(WC)=Wild card. (Q)=Qualifier. (LL)=Lucky loser.

EVENT 9 – THE GIRLS' DOUBLES CHAMPIONSHIP 2017
Holders: USUE MAITANE ARCONADA (USA) & CLAIRE LIU (USA)

The Champions will become the holders, for the year only, of a Cup presented by The All England Lawn Tennis and Croquet Club. The Champions will receive a three-quarter size Cup and the Runners-up will receive Silver Salvers.
The matches will be the best of three sets.

Heavy type denotes seeded players. The figure in brackets against names denotes the order in which they have been seeded. The Committee reserves the right to alter the seeding order in the event of withdrawals.
(WC)=Wild cards. (A)=Alternates.

EVENT 10 – THE GENTLEMEN'S WHEELCHAIR SINGLES 2017
Holder: GORDON REID (GBR)

The Champion will become the holder, for the year only, of a Cup presented by The All England Lawn Tennis and Croquet Club. The Champion will receive a Silver Salver. A Silver Medal will be presented to the Runner-up.
The matches will be the best of three tie-break sets.

First Round	Semi-final	Final	
1. **Gordon Reid [1]** *(1)* .... (GBR)	Stefan Olsson		
2. Stefan Olsson *(7)* .... (SWE)	6/2 6/3	Stefan Olsson	
(WC) 3. Shingo Kunieda *(9)* .... (JPN)	Shingo Kunieda	6/4 6/2	
4. Maikel Scheffers *(8)* .... (NED)	6/3 6/2		Stefan Olsson
5. Alfie Hewett *(6)* .... (GBR)	Alfie Hewett		7/5 3/6 7/5
6. Nicolas Peifer *(5)* .... (FRA)	4/6 6/2 6/2	**Gustavo Fernandez [2]**	
7. Stephane Houdet *(3)* .... (FRA)	**Gustavo Fernandez [2]**	4/6 7/6(4) 6/3	
8. **Gustavo Fernandez [2]** *(2)* .... (ARG)	6/2 6/4		

Heavy type denotes seeded players. The figure in brackets against names denotes the order in which they have been seeded. The Committee reserves the right to alter the seeding order in the event of withdrawals.
(WC)=Wild cards. (A)=Alternates.

EVENT 11 – THE GENTLEMEN'S WHEELCHAIR DOUBLES 2017
Holders: ALFIE HEWETT (GBR) & GORDON REID (GBR)

The Champion will become the holder, for the year only, of a Cup presented by The All England Lawn Tennis and Croquet Club. The Champion will receive a Silver Salver. A Silver Medal will be presented to the Runner-up.
The matches will be the best of three tie-break sets.

First Round	Final	
1. **Stephane Houdet** (FRA) & **Nicolas Peifer** (FRA) .... **[1]**	Stephane Houdet & Nicolas Peifer [1]	
2. Stefan Olsson (SWE) & Maikel Scheffers (NED)	6/4 2/6 6/2	Alfie Hewett & Gordon Reid [2]
3. Gustavo Fernandez (ARG) & Shingo Kunieda (JPN)	Alfie Hewett & Gordon Reid [2]	6/7(5) 7/5 7/6(3)
4. **Alfie Hewett** (GBR) & **Gordon Reid** (GBR) .... **[2]**	6/4 4/6 6/2	

Heavy type denotes seeded players. The figure in brackets against names denotes the order in which they have been seeded. The Committee reserves the right to alter the seeding order in the event of withdrawals.
(WC)=Wild cards. (A)=Alternates.

EVENT 12 – THE LADIES' WHEELCHAIR SINGLES 2017
Holders: JISKE GRIFFIOEN (NED)

The Champion will become the holder, for the year only, of a Cup presented by The All England Lawn Tennis and Croquet Club. The Champion will receive a Silver Salver. A Silver Medal will be presented to the Runner-up.
The matches will be the best of three tie-break sets.

First Round	Semi-final	Final	
1. **Jiske Griffioen [1]** *(1)* .... (NED)	Aniek Van Koot		
2. Aniek Van Koot *(4)* .... (NED)	6/3 6/2	Diede De Groot	
3. Jordanne Whiley *(10)* .... (GBR)	Diede De Groot	6/0 6/2	
4. Diede De Groot *(3)* .... (NED)	6/2 7/6(4)		Diede De Groot
5. Marjolein Buis *(5)* .... (NED)	Sabine Ellerbrock		6/0 6/4
6. Sabine Ellerbrock *(6)* .... (GER)	4/6 7/6(6) 6/4	Sabine Ellerbrock	
(WC) 7. Lucy Shuker *(7)* .... (GBR)	**Yui Kamiji [2]**	7/6(4) 1/6 7/6(4)	
8. **Yui Kamiji [2]** *(2)* .... (JPN)	6/3 6/1		

Heavy type denotes seeded players. The figure in brackets against names denotes the order in which they have been seeded. The Committee reserves the right to alter the seeding order in the event of withdrawals.
(WC)=Wild cards. (A)=Alternates.

EVENT 13 – THE LADIES' WHEELCHAIR DOUBLES 2017
Holders: YUI KAMIJI (JPN) & JORDANNE WHILEY (GBR)

The Champion will become the holder, for the year only, of a Cup presented by The All England Lawn Tennis and Croquet Club. The Champion will receive a Silver Salver. A Silver Medal will be presented to the Runner-up.
The matches will be the best of three tie-break sets.

First Round	Final	
(A) 1. Dana Mathewson (USA) & Aniek Van Koot (NED)	Yui Kamiji & Jordanne Whiley	
2. Yui Kamiji (JPN) & Jordanne Whiley (GBR)	6/4 6/4	Yui Kamiji & Jordanne Whiley
3. Sabine Ellerbrock (GER) & Lucy Shuker (GBR)	**Marjolein Buis & Diede De Groot [2]**	2/6 6/3 6/0
4. **Marjolein Buis** (NED) & **Diede De Groot** (NED) .... **[2]**	6/4 6/1	

Heavy type denotes seeded players. The figure in brackets against names denotes the order in which they have been seeded. The Committee reserves the right to alter the seeding order in the event of withdrawals.
(WC)=Wild cards. (A)=Alternates.

EVENT 14 – THE GENTLEMEN'S INVITATION DOUBLES 2017
Holders: GREG RUSEDSKI (GBR) & FABRICE SANTORO (FRA)

The Champions will become the holders, for the year only, of a Cup presented by The All England Lawn Tennis and Croquet Club. The Champions will receive a silver three-quarter size Cup. A Silver Medal will be presented to each of the Runners-up.
The matches will be the best of three sets. If a match should reach one set all a 10-point tie-break will replace the third set.

GROUP A	Jamie Baker (GBR) & Colin Fleming (GBR)	Mansour Bahrami (IRI) & Michael Llodra (FRA)	Lleyton Hewitt (AUS) & Mark Philippoussis (AUS)	Greg Rusedski (GBR) & Fabrice Santoro (FRA)	Results Wins	Results Losses	Final
Jamie Baker (GBR) & Colin Fleming (GBR)		4/6 4/6 L	6/4 2/6 [6-10] L	6/7(3) 5/7 L	0	3	
Mansour Bahrami (IRI) & Michael Llodra (FRA)	*6/4 6/4		4/6 6/4[7-10] L	4/6 6/3 [7-10] L	0	2	Lleyton Hewitt (AUS) & Mark Philippoussis (AUS) 6/3 6/3
Lleyton Hewitt (AUS) & Mark Philippoussis (AUS)	4/6 6/2 [10-6] W	6/4 4/6 [10-7] W		4/6 7/5 [15-13] W	3	0	
Greg Rusedski (GBR) & Fabrice Santoro (FRA)	7/6(3) 7/5 W	6/4 3/6 [10-7] W	6/4 5/7 [13-15] L		2	1	

*Group A Arnaud Clement (FRA) withdrew (non injury) after first match and was replaced by Mansour Bahrami (IRI). This result does not count towards total matches won.

GROUP B	Mario Ancic (CRO) & Jamie Delgado (GBR)	Thomas Enqvist (SWE) & Thomas Johansson (SWE)	Justin Gimelstob (USA) & Ross Hutchins (GBR)	Fernando Gonzalez (CHI) & Sebastien Grosjean (FRA)	Results Wins	Results Losses	Final
Mario Ancic (CRO) & Jamie Delgado (GBR)		7/5 4/6 [13-11] W	2/6 5/7 L	6/7(3) 6/4 [6-10] L	1	2	
Thomas Enqvist (SWE) & Thomas Johansson (SWE)	5/7 6/4 [11-13] L		6/4 6/3 W	7/6(4) 3/6 [11-13] L	1	2	Justin Gimelstob (USA) & Ross Hutchins (GBR)
Justin Gimelstob (USA) & Ross Hutchins (GBR)	6/2 7/5 W	4/6 3/6 L		6/3 7/5 W	2	1	
Fernando Gonzalez (CHI) & Sebastien Grosjean (FRA)	7/6(3) 4/6 [10-6] W	6/7(4) 6/3 [13-11] W	3/6 5/7 L		2	1	

This event consists of eight invited pairs divided into two groups, playing each other within their group on a 'round robin' basis. The group winner is the pair with the highest number of wins.
In the case of a tie the winning pair may be determined by head to head results or a formula based on percentage of sets/games won to those played.

EVENT 15 – THE GENTLEMEN'S SENIOR INVITATION DOUBLES 2017
Holders: TODD WOODBRIDGE (AUS) & MARK WOODFORDE (AUS)

The Champions will become the holders, for the year only, of a Cup presented by The All England Lawn Tennis and Croquet Club. The Champions will receive a silver half-size Cup. A Silver Medal will be presented to each of the Runners-up.
The matches will be the best of three sets. If a match should reach one set all a 10-point tie-break will replace the third set.

GROUP A	Jeremy Bates (GBR) & Chris Wilkinson (GBR)	Wayne Ferreira (RSA) & Goran Ivanisevic (CRO)	Richard Krajicek (NED) & Mark Petchey (GBR)	Todd Woodbridge (AUS) & Mark Woodforde (AUS)	Results Wins	Results Losses	Final
Jeremy Bates (GBR) & Chris Wilkinson (GBR)		4/6 6/2 [12-10] W	4/6 3/6 L	5/7 6/7(1) L	1	2	
Wayne Ferreira (RSA) & Goran Ivanisevic (CRO)	6/4 2/6 [10-12] L		3/6 6/4[4-10] L	6/2 7/5 W	1	2	Richard Krajicek (NED) & Mark Petchey (GBR)
Richard Krajicek (NED) & Mark Petchey (GBR)	6/4 6/3 W	6/3 4/6 [10-4] W		6/1 6/7(6) [10-7] W	3	0	
Todd Woodbridge (AUS) & Mark Woodforde (AUS)	7/5 7/6(1) W	2/6 5/7 L	1/6 7/6(6)[7-10] L		1	2	

GROUP B	Andrew Castle (GBR) & Michael Chang (USA)	Jacco Eltingh (NED) & Paul Haarhuis (NED)	Henri Leconte (FRA) & Cedric Pioline (FRA)	Patrick McEnroe (USA) & Jeff Tarango (USA)	Results Wins	Results Losses	Final
Andrew Castle (GBR) & Michael Chang (USA)		4/6 4/6 L	6/7(4) 6/2 [7-10] L	7/5 6/3 W	1	2	
Jacco Eltingh (NED) & Paul Haarhuis (NED)	6/4 6/4 W		6/3 6/4 W	4/6 6/3 [10-5] W	3	0	Jacco Eltingh (NED) & Paul Haarhuis (NED) 4/6 6/3 [10-6]
Henri Leconte (FRA) & Cedric Pioline (FRA)	7/6(4) 2/6 [10-7] W	3/6 4/6 L		6/7(3) 6/2 [12-10] W	2	1	
Patrick McEnroe (USA) & Jeff Tarango (USA)	5/7 3/6 L	6/4 3/6 [5-10] L	7/6(3) 2/6 [10-12] L		0	3	

This event consists of eight invited pairs divided into two groups, playing each other within their group on a 'round robin' basis. The group winner is the pair with the highest number of wins.
In the case of a tie the winning pair may be determined by head to head results or a formula based on percentage of sets/games won to those played.

EVENT 16 – THE LADIES' INVITATION DOUBLES 2017
Holders: MARTINA NAVRATILOVA (USA) & SELIMA SFAR (TUN)

The Champions will become the holders, for the year only, of a Cup presented by The All England Lawn Tennis and Croquet Club. The Champions will receive a silver three-quarter size Cup. A Silver Medal will be presented to each of the Runners-up.
The matches will be the best of three sets. If a match should reach one set all a 10-point tie-break will replace the third set.

GROUP A	Tracy Austin (USA) & Helena Sukova (CZE)	Cara Black (ZIM) & Martina Navratilova (USA)	Kim Clijsters (BEL) & Rennae Stubbs (AUS)	Andrea Jaeger (USA) & Conchita Martinez (ESP)	Results Wins	Results Losses	Final
Tracy Austin (USA) & Helena Sukova (CZE)		3/6 4/6 L	1/6 2/6 L	3/6 6/3 [10-4] W	1	2	
Cara Black (ZIM) & Martina Navratilova (USA)	6/3 6/4 W		6/3 6/4 W	6/3 6/1 W	3	0	
Kim Clijsters (BEL) & Rennae Stubbs (AUS)	6/1 6/2 W	3/6 4/6 L		6/2 7/5 W	2	1	
Andrea Jaeger (USA) & Conchita Martinez (ESP)	6/3 3/6 [4-10] L	3/6 1/6 L	2/6 5/7 L		0	3	

Cara Black (ZIM) & Martina Navratilova (USA)

GROUP B	Marion Bartoli (FRA) & Iva Majoli (CRO)	Lindsay Davenport (USA) & Mary Joe Fernandez (USA)	Magdalena Maleeva (BUL) & Barbara Schett (AUT)	Arantxa Sanchez Vicario (ESP) & Selima Sfar (TUN)	Results Wins	Results Losses
Marion Bartoli (FRA) & Iva Majoli (CRO)		2/6 2/6 L	1/6 2/6 L	3/6 0/6 L	0	3
Lindsay Davenport (USA) & Mary Joe Fernandez (USA)	6/2 6/2 W		6/4 6/1	6/4 4/6 [3-10] L	2	1
Magdalena Maleeva (BUL) & Barbara Schett (AUT)	6/1 6/2 W	4/6 1/6 L		2/6 6/1 [8-10] L	1	2
Arantxa Sanchez Vicario (ESP) & Selima Sfar (TUN)	6/3 6/0 W	4/6 6/4 [10-3] W	6/2 1/6 [10-8] W		3	0

Arantxa Sanchez Vicario (ESP) & Selima Sfar (TUN)

Final: Cara Black (ZIM) & Martina Navratilova (USA) 6/2 4/6 [10-4]

This event consists of eight invited pairs divided into two groups, playing each other within their group on a 'round robin' basis. The group winner is the pair with the highest number of wins.
In the case of a tie the winning pair may be determined by head to head results or a formula based on percentage of sets/games won to those played.

COUNTRIES IN THE CHAMPIONSHIPS 2017 – ABBREVIATIONS

ARG .... Argentina	DOM .... Dominican Republic	KOR .... South Korea	RUS .... Russia
AUS .... Australia	ESP .... Spain	LAT .... Latvia	SLO .... Slovenia
AUT .... Austria	EST .... Estonia	LTU .... Lithuania	SRB .... Serbia
BEL .... Belgium	FIN .... Finland	LUX .... Luxembourg	SVK .... Slovakia
BLR .... Belarus	FRA .... France	MEX .... Mexico	RSA .... South Africa
BIH .... Bosnia-Herzegovina	GBR .... Great Britain	MDA .... Moldova	SUI .... Switzerland
BRA .... Brazil	GEO .... Georgia	MNE .... Montenegro	SWE .... Sweden
BUL .... Bulgaria	GER .... Germany	NED .... Netherlands	THA .... Thailand
CAN .... Canada	GRE .... Greece	NZL .... New Zealand	TPE .... Chinese Taipei
CHI .... Chile	HUN .... Hungary	PAK .... Pakistan	TUN .... Tunisia
CHN .... China	IND .... India	PNG .... Papua New Guinea	TUR .... Turkey
COL .... Colombia	IRI .... Iran	PAR .... Paraguay	UKR .... Ukraine
CRO .... Croatia	IRL .... Ireland	PHI .... Philippines	URU .... Uruguay
CYP .... Cyprus	ISR .... Israel	POL .... Poland	USA .... USA
CZE .... Czech Republic	ITA .... Italy	POR .... Portugal	UZB .... Uzbekistan
DEN .... Denmark	JPN .... Japan	PUR .... Puerto Rico	ZIM .... Zimbabwe
	KAZ .... Kazakhstan	ROU .... Romania	

ROLLS OF HONOUR
GENTLEMEN'S SINGLES CHAMPIONS & RUNNERS-UP

1877 S.W.Gore *W.C.Marshall*	1904 H.L.Doherty *F.L.Riseley*	1935 F.J.Perry *G.von Cramm*	1968 R.G.Laver *A.D.Roche*	1995 P.Sampras *B.F.Becker*
1878 P.F.Hadow *S.W.Gore*	1905 H.L.Doherty *N.E.Brookes*	1936 F.J.Perry *G.von Cramm*	1969 R.G.Laver *J.D.Newcombe*	1996 R.P.S.Krajicek *M.O.Washington*
*1879 J.T.Hartley *V.T.St.L.Goold*	1906 H.L.Doherty *F.L.Riseley*	*1937 J.D.Budge *G.von Cramm*	1970 J.D.Newcombe *K.R.Rosewall*	1997 P.Sampras *C.A.Pioline*
1880 J.T.Hartley *H.F.Lawford*	*1907 N.E.Brookes *A.W.Gore*	1938 J.D.Budge *H.W.Austin*	1971 J.D.Newcombe *S.R.Smith*	1998 P.Sampras *G.S.Ivanisevic*
1881 W.C.Renshaw *J.T.Hartley*	*1908 A.W.Gore *H.R.Barrett*	*1939 R.L.Riggs *E.T.Cooke*	*1972 S.R.Smith *I.Nastase*	1999 P.Sampras *A.K.Agassi*
1882 W.C.Renshaw *J.E.Renshaw*	1909 A.W.Gore *M.J.G.Ritchie*	*1946 Y.F.M.Petra *G.E.Brown*	*1973 J.Kodes *A.Metreveli*	2000 P.Sampras *P.M.Rafter*
1883 W.C.Renshaw *J.E.Renshaw*	1910 A.F.Wilding *A.W.Gore*	1947 J.A.Kramer *T.P.Brown*	1974 J.S.Connors *K.R.Rosewall*	2001 G.Ivanisevic *P.M.Rafter*
1884 W.C.Renshaw *H.F.Lawford*	1911 A.F.Wilding *H.R.Barrett*	*1948 R.Falkenburg *J.E.Bromwich*	1975 A.R.Ashe *J.S.Connors*	2002 L.G.Hewitt *D.P.Nalbandian*
1885 W.C.Renshaw *H.F.Lawford*	1912 A.F.Wilding *A.W.Gore*	1949 F.R.Schroeder *J.Drobny*	1976 B.R.Borg *I.Nastase*	2003 R.Federer *M.A.Philippoussis*
1886 W.C.Renshaw *H.F.Lawford*	1913 A.F.Wilding *M.E.McLoughlin*	*1950 J.E.Patty *F.A.Sedgman*	1977 B.R.Borg *J.S.Connors*	2004 R.Federer *A.S.Roddick*
*1887 H.F.Lawford *J.E.Renshaw*	1914 N.E.Brookes *A.F.Wilding*	1951 R.Savitt *K.B.McGregor*	1978 B.R.Borg *J.S.Connors*	2005 R.Federer *A.S.Roddick*
1888 J.E.Renshaw *H.F.Lawford*	1919 G.L.Patterson *N.E.Brookes*	1952 F.A.Sedgman *J.Drobny*	1979 B.R.Borg *L.R.Tanner*	2006 R.Federer *R.Nadal*
1889 W.C.Renshaw *J.E.Renshaw*	1920 W.T.Tilden *G.L.Patterson*	*1953 E.V.Seixas *K.Nielsen*	1980 B.Borg *J.P.McEnroe*	2007 R.Federer *R.Nadal*
1890 W.J.Hamilton *W.C.Renshaw*	1921 W.T.Tilden *B.I.C.Norton*	1954 J.Drobny *K.R.Rosewall*	1981 J.P.McEnroe *B.R.Borg*	2008 R.Nadal *R.Federer*
*1891 W.Baddeley *J.Pim*	*†1922 G.L.Patterson *R.Lycett*	1955 M.A.Trabert *K.Nielsen*	1982 J.S.Connors *J.P.McEnroe*	2009 R.Federer *A.S.Roddick*
1892 W.Baddeley *J.Pim*	*1923 W.M.Johnston *F.T.Hunter*	*1956 L.A.Hoad *K.R.Rosewall*	1983 J.P.McEnroe *C.J.Lewis*	2010 R.Nadal *T.Berdych*
1893 J.Pim *W.Baddeley*	*1924 J.R.Borotra *J.R.Lacoste*	1957 L.A.Hoad *A.J.Cooper*	1984 J.P.McEnroe *J.S.Connors*	2011 N.Djokovic *R.Nadal*
1894 J.Pim *W.Baddeley*	1925 J.R.Lacoste *J.R.Borotra*	*1958 A.J.Cooper *N.A.Fraser*	1985 B.F.Becker *K.M.Curren*	2012 R.Federer *A.B.Murray*
*1895 W.Baddeley *W.V.Eaves*	*1926 J.R.Borotra *H.O.Kinsey*	*1959 A.R.Olmedo *R.G.Laver*	1986 B.F.Becker *I.Lendl*	2013 A.B.Murray *N.Djokovic*
1896 H.S.Mahony *W.Baddeley*	1927 H.J.Cochet *J.R.Borotra*	*1960 N.A.Fraser *R.G.Laver*	1987 P.H.Cash *I.Lendl*	2014 N.Djokovic *R.Federer*
1897 R.F.Doherty *H.S.Mahony*	1928 J.R.Lacoste *H.J.Cochet*	1961 R.G.Laver *C.R.McKinley*	1988 S.B.Edberg *B.F.Becker*	2015 N.Djokovic *R.Federer*
1898 R.F.Doherty *H.L.Doherty*	*1929 H.J.Cochet *J.R.Borotra*	1962 R.G.Laver *M.F.Mulligan*	1989 B.F.Becker *S.B.Edberg*	2016 A.B.Murray *M.Raonic*
1899 R.F.Doherty *A.W.Gore*	1930 W.T.Tilden *W.L.Allison*	*1963 C.R.McKinley *F.S.Stolle*	1990 S.B.Edberg *B.F.Becker*	2017 R.Federer *M.Cilic*
1900 R.F.Doherty *S.H.Smith*	*1931 S.B.B.Wood *F.X.Shields*	1964 R.S.Emerson *F.S.Stolle*	1991 M.D.Stich *B.F.Becker*	
1901 A.W.Gore *R.F.Doherty*	1932 H.E.Vines *H.W.Austin*	1965 R.S.Emerson *F.S.Stolle*	1992 A.K.Agassi *G.S.Ivanisevic*	
1902 H.L.Doherty *A.W.Gore*	1933 J.H.Crawford *H.E.Vines*	1966 M.M.Santana *R.D.Ralston*	1993 P.Sampras *J.S.Courier*	
1903 H.L.Doherty *F.L.Riseley*	1934 F.J.Perry *J.H.Crawford*	1967 J.D.Newcombe *W.P.Bungert*	1994 P.Sampras *G.S.Ivanisevic*	

For the years 1913, 1914 and 1919-1923 inclusive the above records include the "World's Championships on Grass" granted to The Lawn Tennis Association by The International Lawn Tennis Federation.
This title was then abolished and commencing in 1924 they became The Official Lawn Tennis Championships recognised by The International Lawn Tennis Federation.
Prior to 1922 the holders in the Singles Events and Gentlemen's Doubles did not compete in The Championships but met the winners of these events in the Challenge Rounds.
† Challenge Round abolished: holders subsequently played through.
* The holder did not defend the title.

LADIES' SINGLES CHAMPIONS & RUNNERS-UP

1884	Miss M.E.E.Watson *Miss L.M.Watson*	1910	Mrs.R.L.Chambers *Miss P.D.H.Boothby*	*1946	Miss P.M.Betz *Miss A.L.Brough*	1972	Mrs.L.W.King *Miss E.F.Goolagong*	*1997	Miss M.Hingis *Miss J.Novotna*
1885	Miss M.E.E.Watson *Miss B.Bingley*	1911	Mrs.R.L.Chambers *Miss P.D.H.Boothby*	*1947	Miss M.E.Osborne *Miss D.J.Hart*	1973	Mrs.L.W.King *Miss C.M.Evert*	1998	Miss J.Novotna *Miss N.Tauziat*
1886	Miss B.Bingley *Miss M.E.E.Watson*	*1912	Mrs.D.T.R.Larcombe *Mrs.A.Sterry*	1948	Miss A.L.Brough *Miss D.J.Hart*	1974	Miss C.M.Evert *Mrs.O.V.Morozova*	1999	Miss L.A.Davenport *Miss S.M.Graf*
1887	Miss C.Dod *Miss B.Bingley*	*1913	Mrs.R.L.Chambers *Mrs.R.J.McNair*	1949	Miss A.L.Brough *Mrs.W.du Pont*	1975	Mrs.L.W.King *Mrs.R.A.Cawley*	2000	Miss V.E.S.Williams *Miss L.A.Davenport*
1888	Miss C.Dod *Mrs.G.W.Hillyard*	1914	Mrs.R.L.Chambers *Mrs.D.T.R.Larcombe*	1950	Miss A.L.Brough *Mrs.W.du Pont*	*1976	Miss C.M.Evert *Mrs.R.A.Cawley*	2001	Miss V.E.S.Williams *Miss J.Henin*
*1889	Mrs.G.W.Hillyard *Miss H.G.B.Rice*	1919	Miss S.R.F.Lenglen *Mrs.R.L.Chambers*	1951	Miss D.J.Hart *Miss S.J.Fry*	1977	Miss S.V.Wade *Miss B.F.Stove*	2002	Miss S.J.Williams *Miss V.E.S.Williams*
*1890	Miss H.G.B.Rice *Miss M.Jacks*	1920	Miss S.R.F.Lenglen *Mrs.R.L.Chambers*	1952	Miss M.C.Connolly *Miss A.L.Brough*	1978	Miss M.Navratilova *Miss C.M.Evert*	2003	Miss S.J.Williams *Miss V.E.S.Williams*
*1891	Miss C.Dod *Mrs.G.W.Hillyard*	1921	Miss S.R.F.Lenglen *Miss E.M.Ryan*	1953	Miss M.C.Connolly *Miss D.J.Hart*	1979	Miss M.Navratilova *Mrs.J.M.Lloyd*	2004	Miss M.Sharapova *Miss S.J.Williams*
1892	Miss C.Dod *Mrs.G.W.Hillyard*	†1922	Miss S.R.F.Lenglen *Mrs.F.I.Mallory*	1954	Miss M.C.Connolly *Miss A.L.Brough*	1980	Mrs.R.A.Cawley *Mrs.J.M.Lloyd*	2005	Miss V.E.S.Williams *Miss L.A.Davenport*
1893	Miss C.Dod *Mrs.G.W.Hillyard*	1923	Miss S.R.F.Lenglen *Miss K.McKane*	*1955	Miss A.L.Brough *Mrs.J.G.Fleitz*	*1981	Mrs.J.M.Lloyd *Miss H.Mandlikova*	2006	Miss A.Mauresmo *Mrs J.Henin-Hardenne*
*1894	Mrs.G.W.Hillyard *Miss E.L.Austin*	1924	Miss K.McKane *Miss H.N.Wills*	1956	Miss S.J.Fry *Miss A.Buxton*	1982	Miss M.Navratilova *Mrs.J.M.Lloyd*	2007	Miss V.E.S.Williams *Miss M.S.Bartoli*
*1895	Miss C.R.Cooper *Miss H.Jackson*	1925	Miss S.R.F.Lenglen *Miss J.C.Fry*	*1957	Miss A.Gibson *Miss D.R.Hard*	1983	Miss M.Navratilova *Miss A.Jaeger*	2008	Miss V.E.S.Williams *Miss S.J.Williams*
1896	Miss C.R.Cooper *Mrs.W.H.Pickering*	1926	Mrs.L.A.Godfree *Miss E.M.de Alvarez*	1958	Miss A.Gibson *Miss F.A.M.Mortimer*	1984	Miss M.Navratilova *Mrs.J.M.Lloyd*	2009	Miss S.J.Williams *Miss V.E.S.Williams*
1897	Mrs.G.W.Hillyard *Miss C.R.Cooper*	1927	Miss H.Wills *Miss E.M.de Alvarez*	*1959	Miss M.E.A.Bueno *Miss D.R.Hard*	1985	Miss M.Navratilova *Mrs.J.M.Lloyd*	2010	Miss S.J.Williams *Miss V.Zvonareva*
*1898	Miss C.R.Cooper *Miss M.L.Martin*	1928	Miss H.N.Wills *Miss E.M.de Alvarez*	1960	Miss M.E.A.Bueno *Miss S.Reynolds*	1986	Miss M.Navratilova *Miss H.Mandlikova*	2011	Miss P.Kvitova *Miss M.Sharapova*
1899	Mrs.G.W.Hillyard *Miss C.R.Cooper*	1929	Miss H.N.Wills *Miss H.H.Jacobs*	*1961	Miss F.A.M.Mortimer *Miss C.C.Truman*	1987	Miss M.Navratilova *Miss S.M.Graf*	2012	Miss S.J.Williams *Miss A.R.Radwanska*
1900	Mrs.G.W.Hillyard *Miss C.R.Cooper*	1930	Mrs.F.S.Moody *Miss E.M.Ryan*	1962	Mrs.J.R.Susman *Mrs.C.Sukova*	1988	Miss S.M.Graf *Miss M.Navratilova*	2013	Miss M.S.Bartoli *Miss S.Lisicki*
1901	Mrs.A.Sterry *Mrs.G.W.Hillyard*	*1931	Miss C.Aussem *Miss H.Krahwinkel*	*1963	Miss M.Smith *Miss B.J.Moffitt*	1989	Miss S.M.Graf *Miss M.Navratilova*	2014	Miss P.Kvitova *Miss E.C.M.Bouchard*
1902	Miss M.E.Robb *Mrs.A.Sterry*	*1932	Mrs.F.S.Moody *Miss H.H.Jacobs*	1964	Miss M.E.A.Bueno *Miss M.Smith*	1990	Miss M.Navratilova *Miss Z.L.Garrison*	2015	Miss S.J.Williams *Miss G.Muguruza*
*1903	Miss D.K.Douglass *Miss E.W.Thomson*	1933	Mrs.F.S.Moody *Miss D.E.Round*	1965	Miss M.Smith *Miss M.E.A.Bueno*	1991	Miss S.M.Graf *Miss G.B.Sabatini*	2016	Miss S.J.Williams *Miss A.Kerber*
1904	Miss D.K.Douglass *Mrs.A.Sterry*	*1934	Miss D.E.Round *Miss H.H.Jacobs*	1966	Mrs.L.W.King *Miss M.E.A.Bueno*	1992	Miss S.M.Graf *Miss M.Seles*	2017	Miss G.Muguruza *Miss V.E.S.Williams*
1905	Miss M.G.Sutton *Miss D.K.Douglass*	1935	Mrs.F.S.Moody *Miss H.H.Jacobs*	1967	Mrs.L.W.King *Mrs.P.F.Jones*	1993	Miss S.M.Graf *Miss J.Novotna*		
1906	Miss D.K.Douglass *Miss M.G.Sutton*	*1936	Miss H.H.Jacobs *Miss S.Sperling*	1968	Mrs.L.W.King *Miss J.A.M.Tegart*	1994	Miss I.C.Martinez *Miss M.Navratilova*		
1907	Miss M.G.Sutton *Mrs.R.L.Chambers*	1937	Mrs.D.E.Round *Miss J.Jedrzejowska*	1969	Mrs.P.F.Jones *Mrs.L.W.King*	1995	Miss S.M.Graf *Miss A.I.M.Sanchez Vicario*		
*1908	Mrs.A.Sterry *Miss A.M.Morton*	*1938	Mrs.F.S.Moody *Miss H.H.Jacobs*	*1970	Mrs.B.M.Court *Mrs.L.W.King*	1996	Miss S.M.Graf *Miss A.I.M.Sanchez Vicario*		
*1909	Miss P.D.H.Boothby *Miss A.M.Morton*	*1939	Miss A.Marble *Miss K.E.Stammers*	1971	Miss E.F.Goolagong *Mrs.B.M.Court*				

MAIDEN NAMES OF LADIES' CHAMPIONS (In the tables the following have been recorded in both married and single identities)

Mrs. R. Cawley	Miss E. F. Goolagong	Mrs. G. W. Hillyard .... Miss B. Bingley	Mrs. G. E. Reid .... Miss K. Melville
Mrs. R. L. Chambers	Miss D. K. Douglass	Mrs. P. F. Jones .... Miss A. S. Haydon	Mrs. P. D. Smylie .... Miss E. M. Sayers
Mrs. B. M. Court	Miss M. Smith	Mrs. L. W. King .... Miss B. J. Moffitt	Mrs. S. Sperling .... Fräulein H Krahwinkel
Mrs. B. C. Covell	Miss P. L. Howkins	Mrs. M. R. King .... Miss P. E. Mudford	Mrs. A. Sterry .... Miss C.R. Cooper
Mrs. D. E. Dalton	Miss J. A. M. Tegart	Mrs. D. R. Larcombe .... Miss E. W. Thomson	Mrs. J. R. Susman .... Miss K. Hantze
Mrs. W. du Pont	Miss M.E. Osborne	Mrs. J. M. Lloyd .... Miss C. M. Evert	
Mrs. L. A. Godfree	Miss K. McKane	Mrs. F. S. Moody .... Miss H.N. Wills	
Mrs. R.L. Cawley	Miss H. F. Gourlay	Mrs. O.V. Morozova .... Miss O.V. Morozova	
Mrs. J. Henin-Hardenne	Miss J. Henin	Mrs. L. E. G. Price .... Miss S. Reynolds	

GENTLEMEN'S DOUBLES CHAMPIONS & RUNNERS-UP

1879 L.R.Erskine and H.F.Lawford
F.Durant and G.E.Tabor

1880 W.C.Renshaw and J.E.Renshaw
O.E.Woodhouse and C.J.Cole

1881 W.C.Renshaw and J.E.Renshaw
W.J.Down and H.Vaughan

1882 J.T.Hartley and R.T.Richardson
J.G.Horn and C.B.Russell

1883 C.W.Grinstead and C.E.Welldon
C.B.Russell and R.T.Milford

1884 W.C.Renshaw and J.E.Renshaw
E.W.Lewis and E.L.Williams

1885 W.C.Renshaw and J.E.Renshaw
C.E.Farrer and A.J.Stanley

1886 W.C.Renshaw and J.E.Renshaw
C.E.Farrer and A.J.Stanley

1887 P.B.Lyon and
H.W.W.Wilberforce
J.H.Crispe and E.Barratt-Smith

1888 W.C.Renshaw and J.E.Renshaw
*P B.Lyon and
H.W.W.Wilberforce*

1889 W.C.Renshaw and J.E.Renshaw
E.W.Lewis and G.W.Hillyard

1890 J.Pim and F.O.Stoker
E.W.Lewis and G.W.Hillyard

1891 W.Baddeley and H.Baddeley
J.Pim and F.O.Stoker

1892 H.S.Barlow and E.W.Lewis
W.Baddeley and H.Baddeley

1893 J.Pim and F.O.Stoker
E.W.Lewis and H.S.Barlow

1894 W.Baddeley and H.Baddeley
H.S.Barlow and C.H.Martin

1895 W.Baddeley and H.Baddeley
E.W.Lewis and W.V.Eaves

1896 W.Baddeley and H.Baddeley
R.F.Doherty and H.A.Nisbet

1897 R.F.Doherty and H.L.Doherty
W.Baddeley and H.Baddeley

1898 R.F.Doherty and H.L.Doherty
H.A.Nisbet and C.Hobart

1899 R.F.Doherty and H.L.Doherty
H.A.Nisbet and C.Hobart

1900 R.F.Doherty and H.L.Doherty
H.R.Barrett and H.A.Nisbet

1901 R.F.Doherty and H.L.Doherty
D.Davis and H.Ward

1902 S.H.Smith and F.L.Riseley
R.F.Doherty and H.L.Doherty

1903 R.F.Doherty and H.L.Doherty
S.H.Smith and F.L.Riseley

1904 R.F.Doherty and H.L.Doherty
S.H.Smith and F.L.Riseley

1905 R.F.Doherty and H.L.Doherty
S.H.Smith and F.L.Riseley

1906 S.H.Smith and F.L.Riseley
R.F.Doherty and H.L.Doherty

1907 N.E.Brookes and A.F.Wilding
B.C.Wright and K.Behr

1908 A.F.Wilding and M.J.G.Ritchie
A.W.Gore and H.R.Barrett

1909 A.W.Gore and H.R.Barrett
S.N.Doust and H.A.Parker

1910 A.F.Wilding and M.J.G.Ritchie
A.W.Gore and H.R.Barrett

1911 M.O.M.Decugis and A.H.Gobert
M.J.G.Ritchie and A.F.Wilding

1912 H.R.Barrett and C.P.Dixon
M.O.Decugis and A.H.Gobert

1913 H.R.Barrett and C.P.Dixon
F.W.Rahe and H.Kleinschroth

1914 N.E.Brookes and A.F.Wilding
H.R.Barrett and C.P.Dixon

1919 R.V.Thomas and P.O.Wood
R.Lycett and R.W.Heath

1920 R.N.Williams and C.S.Garland
A.R.F.Kingscote and J.C.Parke

1921 R.Lycett and M.Woosnam
F.G.Lowe and A.H.Lowe

1922 R.Lycett and J.O.Anderson
G.L.Patterson and P.O.Wood

1923 R.Lycett and L.A.Godfree
*Count M.de Gomar and
E.Flaquer*

1924 F.T.Hunter and V.Richards
*R.N.Williams and
W.M.Washburn*

1925 J.R.Borotra and R.Lacoste
J.F.Hennessey and R.J.Casey

1926 H.J.Cochet and J.Brugnon
V.Richards and H.O.Kinsey

1927 F.T.Hunter and W.T.Tilden
J.Brugnon and H.J.Cochet

1928 H.J.Cochet and J.Brugnon
G.L.Patterson and J.B.Hawkes

1929 W.L.Allison and J.W.Van Ryn
J.C.Gregory and I.G.Collins

1930 W.L.Allison and J.W.Van Ryn
J.T.G.H.Doeg and G.M.Lott

1931 G.M Lott and J.W.Van Ryn
H.J.Cochet and J.Brugnon

1932 J.R.Borotra and J.Brugnon
G.P.Hughes and F.J.Perry

1933 J.R.Borotra and J.Brugnon
R.Nunoi and J.Satoh

1934 G.M.Lott and L.R.Stoefen
J.R.Borotra and J.Brugnon

1935 J.H.Crawford and A.K.Quist
W.L.Allison and J.W.Van Ryn

1936 G.P.Hughes and C.R.D.Tuckey
C.E.Hare and F.H.D.Wilde

1937 J.D.Budge and G.C.Mako
G.P.Hughes and C.R.D.Tuckey

1938 J.D.Budge and G.C.Mako
H.E.O.Henkel and G.von Metaxa

1939 R.L.Riggs and E.T.Cooke
C.E.Hare and F.H.D.Wilde

1946 T.P.Brown and J.A.Kramer
G.E.Brown and D.R.Pails

1947 R.Falkenburg and J.A.Kramer
A.J.Mottram and O.W.T.Sidwell

1948 J.E.Bromwich and F.A.Sedgman
T.P.Brown and G.P.Mulloy

1949 R.A.Gonzales and F.A.Parker
G.P.Mulloy and F.R.Schroeder

1950 J.E.Bromwich and A.K.Quist
G.E.Brown and O.W.T.Sidwell

1951 K.B.McGregor and F.A.Sedgman
J.Drobny and E.W.Sturgess

1952 K.B.McGregor and F.A.Sedgman
E.V.Seixas and E.W.Sturgess

1953 L.A.Hoad and K.R.Rosewall
R.N.Hartwig and M.G.Rose

1954 R.N.Hartwig and M.G.Rose
E.V.Seixas and M.A.Trabert

1955 R.N.Hartwig and L.A.Hoad
N.A.Fraser and K.R.Rosewall

1956 L.A.Hoad and K.R.Rosewall
N.Pietrangeli and O.Sirola

1957 G.P.Mulloy and J.E.Patty
N.A.Fraser and L.A.Hoad

1958 S.V.Davidson and U.C.J.Schmidt
A.J.Cooper and N.A.Fraser

1959 R.S.Emerson and N.A.Fraser
R.G.Laver and R.Mark

1960 R.H.Osuna and R.D.Ralston
M.G.Davies and R.K.Wilson

1961 R.S.Emerson and N.A.Fraser
R.A.J.Hewitt and F.S.Stolle

1962 R.A.J.Hewitt and F.S.Stolle
B.Jovanovic and N.Pilic

1963 R.H.Osuna and A.Palafox
J.C.Barclay and P.Darmon

1964 R.A.J.Hewitt and F.S.Stolle
R.S.Emerson and K.N.Fletcher

1965 J.D.Newcombe and A.D.Roche
K.N.Fletcher and R.A.J.Hewitt

1966 K.N.Fletcher and J.D.Newcombe
W.W.Bowrey and O.K.Davidson

1967 R.A.J.Hewitt and F.D.McMillan
R.S.Emerson and K.N.Fletcher

1968 J.D.Newcombe and A.D.Roche
K.R.Rosewall and F.S.Stolle

1969 J.D.Newcombe and A.D.Roche
T.S.Okker and M.C.Reissen

1970 J.D.Newcombe and A.D.Roche
K.R.Rosewall and F.S.Stolle

1971 R.S.Emerson and R.G.Laver
A.R.Ashe and R.D.Ralston

1972 R.A.J.Hewitt and F.D.McMillan
S.R.Smith and E.J.van Dillen

1973 J.S.Connors and I.Nastase
J.R.Cooper and N.A.Fraser

1974 J.D.Newcombe and A.D.Roche
R.C.Lutz and S.R.Smith

1975 V.K.Gerulaitis and A.Mayer
C.Dowdeswell and A.J.Stone

1976 B.E.Gottfried and R.C.Ramirez
R.L.Case and G.Masters

1977 R.L.Case and G.Masters
J.G.Alexander and P.C.Dent

1978 R.A.J.Hewitt and F.D.McMillan
P.B.Fleming and J.P.McEnroe

1979 P.B.Fleming and J.P.McEnroe
B.E.Gottfried and R.C.Ramirez

1980 P.McNamara and P.F.McNamee
R.C.Lutz and S.R.Smith

1981 P.B.Fleming and J.P.McEnroe
R.C.Lutz and S.R.Smith

1982 P.McNamara and P.F.McNamee
P.B.Fleming and J.P.McEnroe

1983 P.B.Fleming and J.P.McEnroe
T.E.Gullikson and T.R.Gullikson

1984 P.B.Fleming and J.P.McEnroe
P.Cash and P.McNamee

1985 H.P.Guenthardt and B.Taroczy
P.H.Cash and J.B.Fitzgerald

1986 T.K.Nystrom and
M.A.O.Wilander
G.W.Donnelly and P.B.Fleming

1987 K.E.Flach and R.A.Seguso
S.Casal and E.Sanchez

1988 K.E.Flach and R.A.Seguso
J.B.Fitzgerald and A.P.Jarryd

1989 J.B.Fitzgerald and A.P.Jarryd
R.D.Leach and J.R.Pugh

1990 R.D.Leach and J.R.Pugh
P.Aldrich and D.T.Visser

1991 J.B.Fitzgerald and A.P.Jarryd
J.A.Frana and L.Lavalle

1992 J.P.McEnroe and M.D.Stich
J.F.Grabb and R.A.Reneberg

1993 T.A.Woodbridge and
M.R.Woodforde
G.D.Connell and P.J.Galbraith

1994 T.A.Woodbridge and
M.R.Woodforde
G.D.Connell and P.J.Galbraith

1995 T.A.Woodbridge and
M.R.Woodforde
R.D.Leach and S.D.Melville

1996 T.A.Woodbridge and
M.R.Woodforde
B.H.Black and G.D.Connell

1997 T.A.Woodbridge and
M.R.Woodforde
J.F.Eltingh and P.V.N.Haarhuis

1998 J.F.Eltingh and P.V.N.Haarhuis
*T.A.Woodbridge and
M.R.Woodforde*

1999 M.S.Bhupathi and L.A.Paes
P.V.N.Haarhuis and J.E.Palmer

2000 T.A.Woodbridge and
M.R.Woodforde
P.V.N.Haarhuis and S.F.Stolle

2001 D.J.Johnson and J.E.Palmer
J.Novak and D.Rikl

2002 J.L.Bjorkman and T.A.
Woodbridge
M.S.Knowles and D.M.Nestor

2003 J.L.Bjorkman and T.A.
Woodbridge
M.S.Bhupathi and M.N.Mirnyi

2004 J.L.Bjorkman and T.A.
Woodbridge
J.Knowle and N.Zimonjic

2005 S.W.I.Huss and W.A.Moodie
R.C.Bryan and M.C.Bryan

2006 R.C.Bryan and M.C.Bryan
F.V.Santoro and N.Zimonjic

2007 A.Clement and M.Llodra
R.C.Bryan and M.C.Bryan

2008 D.M.Nestor and N.Zimonjic
J.L.Bjorkman and K.R.Ullyett

2009 D.M.Nestor and N.Zimonjic
R.C.Bryan and M.C.Bryan

2010 J.Melzer and P.Petzschner
R.S.Lindstedt and H.V.Tecau

2011 R.C.Bryan and M.C.Bryan
R.S.Lindstedt and H.V.Tecau

2012 J.F.Marray and F.L.Nielsen
R.S.Lindstedt and H.V.Tecau

2013 R.C.Bryan and M.C.Bryan
I.Dodig and M.P.D.Melo

2014 V.Pospisil and J.E.Sock
R.C.Bryan and M.C.Bryan

2015 J.J.Rojer and H.Tecau
J.R.Murray and J.Peers

2016 P-H.Herbert and N.P.A.Mahut
*J.Benneteau and E.Roger-
Vasselin*

2017 L.Kubot and M.P.D.Melo
O.Marach and M.Pavic

LADIES' DOUBLES CHAMPIONS & RUNNERS-UP

1913	Mrs.R.J.McNair and Miss P.D.H.Boothby *Mrs.A.Sterry and Mrs.R.L.Chambers*		1958	Miss M.E.A.Bueno and Miss A.Gibson *Mrs.W.du Pont and Miss M.Varner*		1993	Miss B.C.Fernandez and Miss N.M.Zvereva *Mrs.A.Neiland and Miss J.Novotna*

1913 Mrs.R.J.McNair and Miss P.D.H.Boothby
Mrs.A.Sterry and Mrs.R.L.Chambers

1914 Miss E.M.Ryan and Miss A.M.Morton
Mrs.D.T.R.Larcombe and Mrs.F.J.Hannam

1919 Miss S.R.F.Lenglen and Miss E.M.Ryan
Mrs.R.L.Chambers and Mrs.D.T.R.Larcombe

1920 Miss S.R.F.Lenglen and Miss E.M.Ryan
Mrs.R.L.Chambers and Mrs.D.T.R.Larcombe

1921 Miss S.R.F.Lenglen and Miss E.M.Ryan
Mrs.A.E.Beamish and Mrs.G.E.Peacock

1922 Miss S.R.F.Lenglen and Miss E.M.Ryan
Mrs.A.D.Stocks and Miss K.McKane

1923 Miss S.R.F.Lenglen and Miss E.M.Ryan
Miss J.W.Austin and Miss E.L.Colyer

1924 Mrs.G.Wightman and Miss H.Wills
Mrs.B.C.Covell and Miss K.McKane

1925 Miss S.Lenglen and Miss E.Ryan
Mrs.A.V.Bridge and Mrs.C.G.McIlquham

1926 Miss E.M.Ryan and Miss M.K.Browne
Mrs.L.A.Godfree and Miss E.L.Colyer

1927 Miss H.N.Wills and Miss E.M.Ryan
Miss E.L.Heine and Mrs.G.E.Peacock

1928 Mrs.M.R.Watson and Miss M.A.Saunders
Miss E.H.Harvey and Miss E.Bennett

1929 Mrs.M.R.Watson and Mrs.L.R.C.Michell
Mrs.B.C.Covell and Mrs.W.P.Barron

1930 Mrs.F.S.Moody and Miss E.M.Ryan
Miss E.A.Cross and Miss S.H.Palfrey

1931 Mrs.D.C.Shepherd-Barron and Miss P.E.Mudford
Miss D.E.Metaxa and Miss J.Sigart

1932 Miss D.E.Metaxa and Miss J.Sigart
Miss E.M.Ryan and Miss H.H.Jacobs

1933 Mrs.R.Mathieu and Miss E.M.Ryan
Miss W.A.James and Miss A.M.Yorke

1934 Mrs.R.Mathieu and Miss E.M.Ryan
Mrs.D.B.Andrus and Mrs.C.F.Henrotin

1935 Miss W.A.James and Miss K.E.Stammers
Mrs.R.Mathieu and Mrs.S.Sperling

1936 Miss W.A.James and Miss K.E.Stammers
Mrs.M.Fabyan and Miss H.H.Jacobs

1937 Mrs.R.Mathieu and Miss A.M.Yorke
Mrs.M.R.King and Mrs.J.B.Pittman

1938 Mrs.M.Fabyan and Miss A.Marble
Mrs.R.Mathieu and Miss A.M.Yorke

1939 Mrs.M.Fabyan and Miss A.Marble
Miss H.H.Jacobs and Miss A.M.Yorke

1946 Miss A.L.Brough and Miss M.E.Osborne
Miss P.M.Betz and Miss D.J.Hart

1947 Miss D.J.Hart and Mrs.R.B.Todd
Miss A.L.Brough and Miss M.E.Osborne

1948 Miss A.L.Brough and Mrs.W.du Pont
Miss D.J.Hart and Mrs.R.B.Todd

1949 Miss A.L.Brough and Mrs.W.du Pont
Miss G.Moran and Mrs.R.B.Todd

1950 Miss A.L.Brough and Mrs.W.du Pont
Miss S.J.Fry and Miss D.J.Hart

1951 Miss S.J.Fry and Miss D.J.Hart
Miss A.L.Brough and Mrs.W.du Pont

1952 Miss S.J.Fry and Miss D.J.Hart
Miss A.L.Brough and Miss M.C.Connolly

1953 Miss S.J.Fry and Miss D.J.Hart
Miss M.C.Connolly and Miss J.A.Sampson

1954 Miss A.L.Brough and Mrs.W.du Pont
Miss S.J.Fry and Miss D.J.Hart

1955 Miss F.A.Mortimer and Miss J.A.Shilcock
Miss S.J.Bloomer and Miss P.E.Ward

1956 Miss A.Buxton and Miss A.Gibson
Miss E.F.Muller and Miss D.G.Seeney

1957 Miss A.Gibson and Miss D.R.Hard
Mrs.K.Hawton and Mrs.M.N.Long

1958 Miss M.E.A.Bueno and Miss A.Gibson
Mrs.W.du Pont and Miss M.Varner

1959 Miss J.M.Arth and Miss D.R.Hard
Mrs.J.G.Fleitz and Miss C.C.Truman

1960 Miss M.E.A.Bueno and Miss D.R.Hard
Miss S.Reynolds and Miss R.Schuurman

1961 Miss K.J.Hantze and Miss B.J.Moffitt
Miss J.P.Lehane and Miss M.Smith

1962 Miss B.J.Moffitt and Mrs.J.R.Susman
Mrs.L.E.G.Price and Miss R.Schuurman

1963 Miss M.E.A.Bueno and Miss D.R.Hard
Miss R.A.Ebbern and Miss M.Smith

1964 Miss M.Smith and Miss L.R.Turner
Miss B.J.Moffitt and Mrs.J.R.Susman

1965 Miss M.E.A.Bueno and Miss B.J.Moffitt
Miss F.G.Durr and Miss J.P.Lieffrig

1966 Miss M.E.A.Bueno and Miss N.A.Richey
Miss M.Smith and Miss J.A.M.Tegart

1967 Miss R.Casals and Mrs.L.W.King
Miss M.E.A.Bueno and Miss N.A.Richey

1968 Miss R.Casals and Mrs.L.W.King
Miss F.G.Durr and Mrs.P.F.Jones

1969 Mrs.B.M.Court and Miss J.A.M.Tegart
Miss P.S.A.Hogan and Miss M.Michel

1970 Miss R.Casals and Mrs.L.W.King
Miss F.G.Durr and Miss S.V.Wade

1971 Miss R.Casals and Mrs.L.W.King
Mrs.B.M.Court and Miss E.F.Goolagong

1972 Mrs.L.W.King and Miss B.F.Stove
Mrs.D.E.Dalton and Miss F.G.Durr

1973 Miss R.Casals and Mrs.L.W.King
Miss F.G.Durr and Miss B.F.Stove

1974 Miss E.F.Goolagong and Miss M.Michel
Miss H.F.Gourlay and Miss K.M.Krantzcke

1975 Miss A.K.Kiyomura and Miss K.Sawamatsu
Miss F.G.Durr and Miss B.F.Stove

1976 Miss C.M.Evert and Miss M.Navratilova
Mrs.L.W.King and Miss B.F.Stove

1977 Mrs.R.L.Cawley and Miss J.C.Russell
Miss M.Navratilova and Miss B.F.Stove

1978 Mrs.G.E.Reid and Miss W.M.Turnbull
Miss M.Jausovec and Miss V.Ruzici

1979 Mrs.L.W.King and Miss M.Navratilova
Miss B.F.Stove and Miss W.M.Turnbull

1980 Miss K.Jordan and Miss A.E.Smith
Miss R.Casals and Miss W.M.Turnbull

1981 Miss M.Navratilova and Miss P.H.Shriver
Miss K.Jordan and Miss A.E.Smith

1982 Miss M.Navratilova and Miss P.H.Shriver
Miss K.Jordan and Miss A.E.Smith

1983 Miss M.Navratilova and Miss P.H.Shriver
Miss R.Casals and Miss W.M.Turnbull

1984 Miss M.Navratilova and Miss P.H.Shriver
Miss K.Jordan and Miss A.E.Smith

1985 Miss K.Jordan and Mrs.P.D.Smylie
Miss M.Navratilova and Miss P.H.Shriver

1986 Miss M.Navratilova and Miss P.H.Shriver
Miss H.Mandlikova and Miss W.M.Turnbull

1987 Miss C.G.Kohde-Kilsch and Miss H.Sukova
Miss H.E.Nagelsen and Mrs.P.D.Smylie

1988 Miss S.M.Graf and Miss G.B.Sabatini
Miss L.I.Savchenko and Miss N.M.Zvereva

1989 Miss J.Novotna and Miss H.Sukova
Miss L.I.Savchenko and Miss N.M.Zvereva

1990 Miss J.Novotna and Miss H.Sukova
Miss K.Jordan and Mrs.P.D.Smylie

1991 Miss L.I.Savchenko and Miss N.M.Zvereva
Miss B.C.Fernandez and Miss J.Novotna

1992 Miss B.C.Fernandez and Miss N.M.Zvereva
Miss J.Novotna and Mrs.A.Neiland

1993 Miss B.C.Fernandez and Miss N.M.Zvereva
Mrs.A.Neiland and Miss J.Novotna

1994 Miss B.C.Fernandez and Miss N.M.Zvereva
Miss J.Novotna and Miss A.I.M.Sanchez Vicario

1995 Miss J.Novotna and Miss A.I.M.Sanchez Vicario
Miss B.C.Fernandez and Miss N.M.Zvereva

1996 Miss M.Hingis and Miss H.Sukova
Miss M.J.McGrath and Mrs.A.Neiland

1997 Miss B.C.Fernandez and Miss N.M.Zvereva
Miss N.J.Arendt and Miss M.M.Bollegraf

1998 Miss M.Hingis and Miss J.Novotna
Miss L.A.Davenport and Miss N.M.Zvereva

1999 Miss L.A.Davenport and Miss C.M.Morariu
Miss M.de Swardt and Miss E.Tatarkova

2000 Miss S.J.Williams and Miss V.E.S.Williams
Mrs.A.Decugis and Miss A.Sugiyama

2001 Miss L.M.Raymond and Miss R.P.Stubbs
Miss K.Clijsters and Miss A.Sugiyama

2002 Miss S.J.Williams and Miss V.E.S.Williams
Miss V.Ruano Pascual and Miss P.L.Suarez

2003 Miss K.Clijsters and Miss A.Sugiyama
Miss V.Ruano Pascual and Miss P.L.Suarez

2004 Miss C.C.Black and Miss R.P.Stubbs
Mrs.A.Huber and Miss A.Sugiyama

2005 Miss C.C.Black and Mrs.A.Huber
Miss S.Kuznetsova and Miss A.Muresmo

2006 Miss Z.Yan and Miss J.Zheng
Miss V.Ruano Pascual and Miss P.L.Suarez

2007 Miss C.C.Black and Mrs.A.Huber
Miss K.Srebotnik and Miss A.Sugiyama

2008 Miss S.J.Williams and Miss V.E.S.Williams
Miss L.M.Raymond and Miss S.J.Stosur

2009 Miss S.J.Williams and Miss V.E.S.Williams
Miss S.J.Stosur and Miss R.P.Stubbs

2010 Miss V.King and Miss Y.V.Shvedova
Miss E.S.Vesnina and Miss V.Zvonareva

2011 Miss K.Peschke and Miss K.Srebotnik
Miss S.Lisicki and Miss S.J.Stosur

2012 Miss S.J.Williams and Miss V.E.S.Williams
Miss A.Hlavackova and Miss L.Hradecka

2013 Miss S-W.Hsieh and Miss S.Peng
Miss A.Barty and Miss C.Dellacqua

2014 Miss S.Errani and Miss R.Vinci
Miss T.Babos and Miss K.Mladenovic

2015 Miss M.Hingis and Miss S.Mirza
Miss E.Makarova and Miss E.S.Vesnina

2016 Miss S.J.Williams and Miss V.E.S.Williams
Miss T.Babos and Miss Y.Shvedova

2017 Miss E.Makarova and Miss E.S.Vesnina
Miss H-C.Chan and Miss M.Niculescu

MIXED DOUBLES CHAMPIONS & RUNNERS-UP

1913	H.Crisp and Mrs.C.O.Tuckey *J.C.Parke and Mrs.D.T.R.Larcombe*	
1914	J.C.Parke and Mrs.D.T.R.Larcombe *A.F.Wilding and Miss M.Broquedis*	
1919	R.Lycett and Miss E.M.Ryan *A.D.Prebble and Mrs.R.L.Chambers*	
1920	G.L.Patterson and Miss S.R.F.Lenglen *R.Lycett and Miss E.M.Ryan*	
1921	R.Lycett and Miss E.M.Ryan *M.Woosnam and Miss P.L.Howkins*	
1922	P.O.Wood and Miss S.R.F.Lenglen *R.Lycett and Miss E.M.Ryan*	
1923	R.Lycett and Miss E.M.Ryan *L.S.Deane and Mrs.W.P.Barron*	

1913 H.Crisp and Mrs.C.O.Tuckey
J.C.Parke and Mrs.D.T.R.Larcombe

1914 J.C.Parke and Mrs.D.T.R.Larcombe
A.F.Wilding and Miss M.Broquedis

1919 R.Lycett and Miss E.M.Ryan
A.D.Prebble and Mrs.R.L.Chambers

1920 G.L.Patterson and Miss S.R.F.Lenglen
R.Lycett and Miss E.M.Ryan

1921 R.Lycett and Miss E.M.Ryan
M.Woosnam and Miss P.L.Howkins

1922 P.O.Wood and Miss S.R.F.Lenglen
R.Lycett and Miss E.M.Ryan

1923 R.Lycett and Miss E.M.Ryan
L.S.Deane and Mrs.W.P.Barron

1924 J.B.Gilbert and Miss K.McKane
L.A.Godfree and Mrs.W.P.Barron

1925 J.Borotra and Miss S.R.F.Lenglen
U.L.de Morpurgo and Miss E.M.Ryan

1926 L.A.Godfree and Mrs.L.A.Godfree
H.O.Kinsey and Miss M.K.Browne

1927 F.T.Hunter and Miss E.M.Ryan
L.A.Godfree and Mrs.L.A.Godfree

1928 P.D.B.Spence and Miss E.M.Ryan
J.H.Crawford and Miss D.J.Akhurst

1929 F.T.Hunter and Miss H.N.Wills
I.G.Collins and Miss J.C.Fry

1930 J.H.Crawford and Miss E.M.Ryan
D.D.Prenn and Miss H.Krahwinkel

1931 G.M.Lott and Mrs.L.A.Harper
I.G.Collins and Miss J.C.Ridley

1932 E.G.Maier and Miss E.M.Ryan
H.C.Hopman and Miss J.Sigart

1933 G.von Cramm and Miss H.Krahwinkel
N.G.Farquharson and Miss G.M.Heeley

1934 R.Miki and Miss D.E.Round
H.W.Austin and Mrs.W.P.Barron

1935 F.J.Perry and Miss D.E.Round
H.C.Hopman and Mrs.H.C.Hopman

1936 F.J.Perry and Miss D.E.Round
J.D.Budge and Mrs.M.Fabyan

1937 J.D.Budge and Miss A.Marble
Y.F.M.Petra and Mrs.R.Mathieu

1938 J.D.Budge and Miss A.Marble
H.E.O.Henkel and Mrs.M.Fabyan

1939 R.L.Riggs and Miss A.Marble
F.H.D.Wilde and Miss N.B.Brown

1946 T.P.Brown and Miss A.L.Brough
G.E.Brown and Miss D.M.Bundy

1947 J.E.Bromwich and Miss A.L.Brough
C.F.Long and Mrs.G.F.Bolton

1948 J.E.Bromwich and Miss A.L.Brough
F.A.Sedgman and Miss D.J.Hart

1949 E.W.Sturgess and Mrs.R.A.Summers
J.E.Bromwich and Miss A.L.Brough

1950 E.W.Sturgess and Miss A.L.Brough
G.E.Brown and Mrs.R.B.Todd

1951 F.A.Sedgman and Miss D.J.Hart
M.G.Rose and Mrs.G.F.Bolton

1952 F.A.Sedgman and Miss D.J.Hart
E.J.Morea and Mrs.M.N.Long

1953 E.V.Seixas and Miss D.J.Hart
E.J.Morea and Miss S.J.Fry

1954 E.V.Seixas and Miss D.J.Hart
K.R.Rosewall and Mrs.W.du Pont

1955 E.V.Seixas and Miss D.J.Hart
E.J.Morea and Miss A.L.Brough

1956 E.V.Seixas and Miss S.J.Fry
G.P.Mulloy and Miss A.Gibson

1957 M.G.Rose and Miss D.R.Hard
N.A.Fraser and Miss A.Gibson

1958 R.N.Howe and Miss L.Coghlan
K.Nielsen and Miss A.Gibson

1959 R.G.Laver and Miss D.R.Hard
N.A.Fraser and Miss M.E.A.Bueno

1960 R.G.Laver and Miss D.R.Hard
R.N.Howe and Miss M.E.A.Bueno

1961 F.S.Stolle and Miss L.R.Turner
R.N.Howe and Miss E.Buding

1962 N.A.Fraser and Mrs.W.du Pont
R.D.Ralston and Miss A.S.Haydon

1963 K.N.Fletcher and Miss M.Smith
R.A.J.Hewitt and Miss D.R.Hard

1964 F.S.Stolle and Miss L.R.Turner
K.N.Fletcher and Miss M.Smith

1965 K.N.Fletcher and Miss M.Smith
A.D.Roche and Miss J.A.M.Tegart

1966 K.N.Fletcher and Miss M.Smith
R.D.Ralston and Mrs.L.W.King

1967 O.K.Davidson and Mrs.L.W.King
K.N.Fletcher and Miss M.E.A.Bueno

1968 K.N.Fletcher and Mrs.B.M.Court
A.Metreveli and Miss O.V.Morozova

1969 F.S.Stolle and Mrs.P.F.Jones
A.D.Roche and Miss J.A.M.Tegart

1970 I.Nastase and Miss R.Casals
A.Metreveli and Miss O.V.Morozova

1971 O.K.Davidson and Mrs.L.W.King
M.C.Riessen and Mrs.B.M.Court

1972 I.Nastase and Miss R.Casals
K.G.Warwick and Miss E.F.Goolagong

1973 O.K.Davidson and Mrs.L.W.King
R.C.Ramirez and Miss J.S.Newberry

1974 O.K.Davidson and Mrs.L.W.King
M.J.Farrell and Miss L.J.Charles

1975 M.C.Riessen and Mrs.B.M.Court
A.J.Stone and Miss B.F.Stove

1976 A.D.Roche and Miss F.G.Durr
R.L.Stockton and Miss R.Casals

1977 R.A.J.Hewitt and Miss G.R.Stevens
F.D.McMillan and Miss B.F.Stove

1978 F.D.McMillan and Miss B.F.Stove
R.O.Ruffels and Mrs.L.W.King

1979 R.A.J.Hewitt and Miss G.R.Stevens
F.D.McMillan and Miss B.F.Stove

1980 J.R.Austin and Miss T.A.Austin
M.R.Edmondson and Miss D.L.Fromholtz

1981 F.D.McMillan and Miss B.F.Stove
J.R.Austin and Miss T.A.Austin

1982 K.M.Curren and Miss A.E.Smith
J.M.Lloyd and Miss W.M.Turnbull

1983 J.M.Lloyd and Miss W.M.Turnbull
S.B.Denton and Mrs.L.W.King

1984 J.M.Lloyd and Miss W.M.Turnbull
S.B.Denton and Miss K.Jordan

1985 P.F.McNamee and Miss M.Navratilova
J.B.Fitzgerald and Mrs.P.D.Smylie

1986 K.E.Flach and Miss K.Jordan
H.P.Guenthardt and Miss M.Navratilova

1987 M.J.Bates and Miss J.M.Durie
D.A.Cahill and Miss N.A-L.Provis

1988 S.E.Stewart and Miss Z.L.Garrison
K.L.Jones and Mrs.S.W.Magers

1989 J.R.Pugh and Miss J.Novotna
M.Kratzmann and Miss J.M.Byrne

1990 R.D.Leach and Miss Z.L.Garrison
J.B.Fitzgerald and Mrs.P.D.Smylie

1991 J.B.Fitzgerald and Mrs.P.D.Smylie
J.R.Pugh and Miss N.M.Zvereva

1992 C.Suk and Mrs.A.Neiland
J.F.Eltingh and Miss M.J.M.M.Oremans

1993 M.R.Woodforde and Miss M.Navratilova
T.J.C.M.Nijssen and Miss M.M.Bollegraf

1994 T.A.Woodbridge and Miss H.Sukova
T.J.Middleton and Miss L.M.McNeil

1995 J.A.Stark and Miss M.Navratilova
C.Suk and Miss B.C.Fernandez

1996 C.Suk and Miss H.Sukova
M.R.Woodforde and Mrs.A.Neiland

1997 C.Suk and Miss H.Sukova
A.Olhovskiy and Mrs.A.Neiland

1998 M.N.Mirnyi and Miss S.J.Williams
M.S.Bhupathi and Miss M.Lucic

1999 L.A.Paes and Miss L.M.Raymond
J.L.Bjorkman and Miss A.S.Kournikova

2000 D.J.Johnson and Miss K.Y.Po
L.G.Hewitt and Miss K.Clijsters

2001 L.Friedl and Miss D.Hantuchova
M.C.Bryan and Mrs.A.Huber

2002 M.S.Bhupathi and Miss E.A.Likhovtseva
K.R.Ullyett and Miss D.Hantuchova

2003 L.A.Paes and Miss M.Navratilova
A.Ram and Miss A.Rodionova

2004 W.Black and Miss C.C.Black
T.A.Woodbridge and Miss A.H.Molik

2005 M.S.Bhupathi and Miss M.C.Pierce
P.Hanley and Miss T.Perebiynis

2006 A.Ram and Miss V.Zvonareva
R.C.Bryan and Miss V.E.S.Williams

2007 J.R.Murray and Miss J.Jankovic
J.L.Bjorkman and Miss A.H.Molik

2008 R.C.Bryan and Miss S.J.Stosur
M.C.Bryan and Miss K.Srebotnik

2009 M.S.Knowles and Miss A-L.Groenefeld
L.A.Paes and Miss C.C.Black

2010 L.A.Paes and Miss C.C.Black
W.A.Moodie and Miss L.M.Raymond

2011 J.Melzer and Miss I.Benesova
M.S.Bhupathi and Miss E.S.Vesnina

2012 M.Bryan and Miss L.M.Raymond
L.A.Paes and Miss E.S.Vesnina

2013 D.M.Nestor and Miss K.Mladenovic
B.Soares and Miss L.M.Raymond

2014 N.Zimonjic and Miss S.J.Stosur
M.N.Mirnyi and Miss H-C.Chan

2015 L.A.Paes and Miss M.Hingis
A.Peya and Miss T.Babos

2016 H.Kontinen and Miss H.M.Watson
R.F.Farah and Miss A-L.Groenefeld

2017 J.R.Murray and Miss M.Hingis
H.Kontinen and Miss H.M.Watson

BOYS' SINGLES CHAMPIONS & RUNNERS-UP

1947 K.Nielsen *S.V.Davidson*	1965 V.Korotkov *G.Goven*	1983 S.B.Edberg *J.Frawley*
1948 S.O.Stockenberg *D.Vad*	1966 V.Korotkov *B.E.Fairlie*	1984 M.Kratzmann *S.Kruger*
1949 S.O.Stockenberg *J.A.T.Horn*	1967 M.Orantes *M.S.Estep*	1985 L.Lavalle *E.Velez*
1950 J.A.T.Horn *K.Mobarek*	1968 J.G.Alexander *J.Thamin*	1986 E.Velez *J.Sanchez*
1951 J.Kupferburger *K.Mobarek*	1969 B.M.Bertram *J.G.Alexander*	1987 D.Nargiso *J.R.Stoltenberg*
1952 R.K.Wilson *T.T.Fancutt*	1970 B.M.Bertram *F.Gebert*	1988 N.Pereira *G.Raoux*
1953 W.A.Knight *R.Krishnan*	1971 R.I.Kreiss *S.A.Warboys*	1989 L.J.N.Kulti *T.A.Woodbridge*
1954 R.Krishnan *A.J.Cooper*	1972 B.R.Borg *C.J.Mottram*	1990 L.A.Paes *M.Ondruska*
1955 M.P.Hann *J.E.Lundquist*	1973 W.W.Martin *C.S.Dowdeswell*	1991 K.J.T.Enquist *M.Joyce*
1956 R.E.Holmberg *R.G.Laver*	1974 W.W.Martin *Ash Amritraj*	1992 D.Skoch *B.Dunn*
1957 J.I.Tattersall *I.Ribeiro*	1975 C.J.Lewis *R.Ycaza*	1993 R.Sabau *J.Szymanski*
1958 E.H.Buchholz *P.J.Lall*	1976 H.P.Guenthardt *P.Elter*	1994 S.M.Humphries *M.A.Philippoussis*
1959 T.Lejus *R.W.Barnes*	1977 V.A.W.Winitsky *T.E.Teltscher*	1995 O.Mutis *N.Kiefer*
1960 A.R.Mandelstam *J.Mukerjea*	1978 I.Lendl *J.Turpin*	1996 V.Voltchkov *I.Ljubicic*
1961 C.E.Graebner *E.Blanke*	1979 R.Krishnan *D.Siegler*	1997 W.Whitehouse *D.Elsner*
1962 S.J.Matthews *A.Metreveli*	1980 T.Tulasne *H.D.Beutel*	1998 R.Federer *I.Labadze*
1963 N.Kalogeropoulos *I.El Shafei*	1981 M.W.Anger *P.H.Cash*	1999 J.Melzer *K.Pless*
1964 I.El Shafei *V.Korotkov*	1982 P.H.Cash *H.Sundstrom*	2000 N.P.A.Mahut *M.Ancic*

2001 R.Valent *G.Muller*
2002 T.C.Reid *L.Quahab*
2003 F.Mergea *C.Guccione*
2004 G.Monfils *M.Kasiri*
2005 J.Chardy *R.Haase*
2006 T.De Bakker *M.Gawron*
2007 D.Young *V.Ignatic*
2008 G.Dimitrov *H.Kontinen*
2009 A.Kuznetsov *J.Cox*
2010 M.Fucsovics *B.Mitchell*
2011 L.Saville *L.Broady*
2012 F.Peliwo *L.Saville*
2013 G.Quinzi *H.Chung*
2014 N.Rubin *S.Kozlov*
2015 R.Opelka *M.Ymer*
2016 D.Shapovalov *A.De Minaur*
2017 A.Davidovich Fokina *A.Geller*

BOYS' DOUBLES CHAMPIONS & RUNNERS-UP

1982 P.H.Cash and J.Frawley *R.D.Leach and J.J.Ross*	1995 J.Lee and J.M.Trotman *A.Hernandez and M.Puerta*	2008 C-P.Hsieh and T-H.Yang *M.Reid and B.Tomic*
1983 M.Kratzmann and S.Youl *M.Nastase and O.Rahnasto*	1996 D.Bracciali and J.Robichaud *D.Roberts and W.Whitehouse*	2009 P-H.Herbert and K.Krawietz *J.Obry and A.Puget*
1984 R.Brown and R.V.Weiss *M.Kratzmann and J.Svensson*	1997 L.Horna and N.Massu *J.Van de Westhuizen and W.Whitehouse*	2010 L.Broady and T.Farquharson *L.Burton and G.Morgan*
1985 A.Moreno and J.Yzaga *P.Korda and C.Suk*	1998 R.Federer and O.L.P.Rochus *M.Llodra and A.Ram*	2011 G.Morgan and M.Pavic *O.Golding and J.Vesely*
1986 T.Carbonell and P.Korda *S.Barr and H.Karrasch*	1999 G.Coria and D.P.Nalbandian *T.Enev and J.Nieminem*	2012 A.Harris and N.Kyrgios *M.Donati and P.Licciardi*
1987 J.Stoltenberg and T.A.Woodbridge *D.Nargiso and E.Rossi*	2000 D.Coene and K.Vliegen *A.Banks and B.Riby*	2013 T.Kokkinakis and N.Kyrgios *E.Couacaud and S.Napolitano*
1988 J.R.Stoltenberg and T.A.Woodbridge *D.Rikl and T.Zdrazila*	2001 F.Dancevic and G.Lapentti *B.Echagaray and S.Gonzales*	2014 O.Luz and M.Zormann *S.Kozlov and A.Rublev*
1989 J.E.Palmer and J.A.Stark *J-L.De Jager and W.R.Ferreira*	2002 F.Mergea and H.V.Tecau *B.Baker and B.Ram*	2015 N.H.Ly and S.Nagal *R.Opelka and A.Santillan*
1990 S.Lareau and S.Leblanc *C.Marsh and M.Ondruska*	2003 F.Mergea and H.V.Tecau *A.Feeney and C.Guccione*	2016 K.Raisma and S.Tsitsipas *F.Auger-Aliassime and D.Shapovalov*
1991 K.Alami and G.Rusedski *J-L.De Jager and A.Medvedev*	2004 B.Evans and S.Oudsema *R.Haase and V.Troicki*	2017 A.Geller and Y.H.Hsu *J.Rodionov and M.Vrbensky*
1992 S.Baldas and S.Draper *M.S.Bhupathi and N.Kirtane*	2005 J.Levine and M.Shabaz *S.Groth and A.Kennaugh*	
1993 S.Downs and J.Greenhalgh *N.Godwin and G.Williams*	2006 K.Damico and N.Schnugg *M.Klizan and A.Martin*	
1994 B.Ellwood and M.Philippoussis *V.Platenik and R.Schlachter*	2007 D.Lopez and M.Trevisan *R.Jebavy and M.Klizan*	

GIRLS' SINGLES CHAMPIONS & RUNNERS-UP

1947 Miss G.Domken
Miss B.Wallen

1948 Miss O.Miskova
Miss V.Rigollet

1949 Miss C.Mercelis
Miss J.S.V.Partridge

1950 Miss L.Cornell
Miss A.Winter

1951 Miss L.Cornell
Miss S.Lazzarino

1952 Miss F.J.I.ten Bosch
Miss R.Davar

1953 Miss D.Kilian
Miss V.A.Pitt

1954 Miss V.A.Pitt
Miss C.Monnot

1955 Miss S.M.Armstrong
Miss B.de Chambure

1956 Miss A.S.Haydon
Miss I.Buding

1957 Miss M.G.Arnold
Miss E.Reyes

1958 Miss S.M.Moore
Miss A.Dmitrieva

1959 Miss J.Cross
Miss D.Schuster

1960 Miss K.J.Hantze
Miss L.M.Hutchings

1961 Miss G.Baksheeva
Miss K.D.Chabot

1962 Miss G.Baksheeva
Miss E.P.Terry

1963 Miss D.M.Salfati
Miss K.Dening

1964 Miss J.M.Bartkowicz
Miss E.Subirats

1965 Miss O.V.Morozova
Miss R.Giscarfe

1966 Miss B.Lindstrom
Miss J.A.Congdon

1967 Miss J.H.Salome
Miss E.M.Strandberg

1968 Miss K.S.Pigeon
Miss L.E.Hunt

1969 Miss K.Sawamatsu
Miss B.I.Kirk

1970 Miss S.A.Walsh
Miss M.V.Kroshina

1971 Miss M.V.Kroschina
Miss S.H.Minford

1972 Miss I.S.Kloss
Miss G.L.Coles

1973 Miss A.K.Kiyomura
Miss M.Navratilova

1974 Miss M.Jausovec
Miss M.Simionescu

1975 Miss N.Y.Chmyreva
Miss R.Marsikova

1976 Miss N.Y.Chmyreva
Miss M.Kruger

1977 Miss L.Antonoplis
Miss M.Louie

1978 Miss T.A.Austin
Miss H.Mandlikova

1979 Miss M.L.Piatek
Miss A.A.Moulton

1980 Miss D.Freeman
Miss S.J.Leo

1981 Miss Z.L.Garrison
Miss R.R.Uys

1982 Miss C.Tanvier
Miss H.Sukova

1983 Miss P.Paradis
Miss P.Hy

1984 Miss A.N.Croft
Miss E.Reinach

1985 Miss A.Holikova
Miss J.M.Byrne

1986 Miss N.M.Zvereva
Miss L.Meskhi

1987 Miss N.M.Zvereva
Miss J.Halard

1988 Miss B.A.M.Schultz
Miss E.Derly

1989 Miss A.Strnadova
Miss M.J.McGrath

1990 Miss A.Strnadova
Miss K.Sharpe

1991 Miss B.Rittner
Miss E.Makarova

1992 Miss C.R.Rubin
Miss L.Courtois

1993 Miss N.Feber
Miss R.Grande

1994 Miss M.Hingis
Miss M-R.Jeon

1995 Miss A.Olsza
Miss T.Tanasugarn

1996 Miss A.Mauresmo
Miss M.L.Serna

1997 Miss C.C.Black
Miss A.Rippner

1998 Miss K.Srebotnik
Miss K.Clijsters

1999 Miss I.Tulyagnova
Miss L.Krasnoroutskaya

2000 Miss M.E.Salerni
Miss T.Perebiynis

2001 Miss A.Widjaja
Miss D.Safina

2002 Miss V.Douchevina
Miss M.Sharapova

2003 Miss K.Flipkens
Miss A.Tchakvetadze

2004 Miss K.Bondarenko
Miss A.Ivanovic

2005 Miss A.R.Radwanska
Miss T.Paszek

2006 Miss C.Wozniacki
Miss M.Rybarikova

2007 Miss U.Radwanska
Miss M.Brengle

2008 Miss L.M.D.Robson
Miss N.Lertcheewakarn

2009 Miss N.Lertcheewakarn
Miss K.Mladenovic

2010 Miss K.Pliskova
Miss S.Ishizu

2011 Miss A.Barty
Miss I.Khromacheva

2012 Miss E.Bouchard
Miss E.Svitolina

2013 Miss B.Bencic
Miss T.Townsend

2014 Miss J.Ostapenko
Miss K.Schmiedlova

2015 Miss S.Zhuk
Miss A.Blinkova

2016 Miss A.S.Potapova
Miss D.O.Yastremska

2017 Miss C.Liu
Miss A.Li

GIRLS' DOUBLES CHAMPIONS & RUNNERS-UP

1982 Miss E.A.Herr and Miss P.Barg
Miss B.S.Gerken and Miss G.A.Rush

1983 Miss P.A.Fendick and Miss P.Hy
Miss C.Anderholm and Miss H.Olsson

1984 Miss C.Kuhlman and Miss S.C.Rehe
Miss V.Milvidskaya and Miss L.I.Savchenko

1985 Miss L.Field and Miss J.G.Thompson
Miss E.Reinach and Miss J.A.Richardson

1986 Miss M.Jaggard and Miss L.O'Neill
Miss L.Meskhi and Miss N.M.Zvereva

1987 Miss N.Medvedeva and Miss N.M.Zvereva
Miss I.S.Kim and Miss P.M.Moreno

1988 Miss J.A.Faull and Miss R.McQuillan
Miss A.Dechaume and Miss E.Derly

1989 Miss J.M.Capriati and Miss M.J.McGrath
Miss A.Strnadova and Miss E.Sviglerova

1990 Miss K.Habsudova and Miss A.Strnadova
Miss N.J.Pratt and Miss K.Sharpe

1991 Miss C.Barclay and Miss L.Zaltz
Miss J.Limmer and Miss A.Woolcock

1992 Miss M.Avotins and Miss L.McShea
Miss P.Nelson and Miss J.Steven

1993 Miss L.Courtois and Miss N.Feber
Miss H.Mochizuki and Miss Y.Yoshida

1994 Miss E.De Villiers and Miss E.E.Jelfs
Miss C.M.Morariu and Miss L.Varmuzova

1995 Miss C.C.Black and Miss A.Olsza
Miss T.Musgrove and Miss J.Richardson

1996 Miss O.Barabanschikova and Miss A.Mauresmo
Miss L.Osterloh and Miss S.Reeves

1997 Miss C.C.Black and Miss I.Selyutina
Miss M.Matevzic and Miss K.Srebotnik

1998 Miss E.Dyrberg and Miss J.Kostanic
Miss P.Rampre and Miss I.Tulyaganova

1999 Miss D.Bedanova and Miss M.E.Salerni
Miss T.Perebiynis and Miss I.Tulyaganova

2000 Miss I.Gaspar and Miss T.Perebiynis
Miss D.Bedanova and Miss M.E.Salerni

2001 Miss G.Dulko and Miss A.Harkleroad
Miss C.Horiatopoulos and Miss B.Mattek

2002 Miss E.Clijsters and Miss B.Strycova
Miss A.Baker and Miss A-L.Groenefeld

2003 Miss A.Kleybanova and Miss S.Mirza
Miss K.Bohmova and Miss M.Krajicek

2004 Miss V.A.Azarenka and Miss V.Havartsova
Miss M.Erakovic and Miss M.Niculescu

2005 Miss V.A.Azarenka and Miss A.Szavay
Miss M.Erakovic and Miss M.Niculescu

2006 Miss A.Kleybanova and Miss A.Pavlyuchenkova
Miss K.Antoniychuk and Miss A.Dulgheru

2007 Miss A.Pavlyuchenkova and Miss U.Radwanska
Miss M.Doi and Miss K.Nara

2008 Miss P.Hercog and Miss J.Moore
Miss I.Holland and Miss S.Peers

2009 Miss N.Lertcheewakarn and Miss S.Peers
Miss K.Mladenovic and Miss S.Njiric

2010 Miss T.Babos and Miss S.Stephens
Miss I.Khromacheva and Miss E.Svitolina

2011 Miss E.Bouchard and Miss G.Min
Miss D.Schuurs and Miss H.C.Tang

2012 Miss E.Bouchard and Miss T.Townsend
Miss B.Bencic and Miss A.Konjuh

2013 Miss B.Krejcikova and Miss K.Siniakova
Miss A.Kalinina and Miss I.Shymanovich

2014 Miss T.Grende and Miss Q.Ye
Miss M.Bouzkova and Miss D.Galfi

2015 Miss D.Galfi and Miss F.Stollar
Miss V.Lapko and Miss T.Mihalikova

2016 Miss U.M.Arconada and Miss C.Liu
Miss M.Bolkvadze and Miss C.McNally

2017 Miss O.Danilovic and Miss K.Juvan
Miss C.McNally and Miss W.Osuigwe

GENTLEMEN'S WHEELCHAIR SINGLES CHAMPIONS & RUNNERS-UP

2016 G.Reid
S.Olsson

2017 S.Olsson
G.Fernandez

GENTLEMEN'S WHEELCHAIR DOUBLES CHAMPIONS & RUNNERS-UP

2006 S.Saida and S.Kunieda
M.Jeremiasz and J.Mistry

2007 R.Ammerlaan and R.Vink
S.Kunieda and S.Saida

2008 R.Ammerlaan and R.Vink
S.Houdet and N.Peifer

2009 S.Houdet and M.Jeremiasz
R.Ammerlaan and S.Kunieda

2010 R.Ammerlaan and S.Olsson
S.Houdet and S.Kunieda

2011 M.Scheffers and R.Vink
S.Houdet and M.Jeremiasz

2012 T.Egberink and M.Jeremiasz
R.Ammerlaan and R.Vink

2013 S.Houdet and S.Kunieda
F.Cattaneo and R.Vink

2014 S.Houdet and S.Kunieda
M.Scheffers and R.Vink

2015 G.Fernandez and N.Peifer
M.Jeremiasz and G.Reid

2016 A.T.Hewett and G.Reid
S.Houdet and N.Peifer

2017 A.T.Hewett and G.Reid
S.Houdet and N.Peifer

LADIES' WHEELCHAIR SINGLES CHAMPIONS & RUNNERS-UP

2016 Miss J.Griffioen
Miss A.van Koot

2017 Miss D.de Groot
Miss S.Ellerbrock

LADIES' WHEELCHAIR DOUBLES CHAMPIONS & RUNNERS-UP

2009 Miss K.Homan and Miss E.M.Vergeer
Miss D.Di Toro and Miss L.Shuker

2010 Miss E.M.Vergeer and Miss S.Walraven
Miss D.Di Toro and Miss L.Shuker

2011 Miss E.M.Vergeer and Miss S.Walraven
Miss J.Griffioen and Miss A.van Koot

2012 Miss J.Griffioen and Miss A.van Koot
Miss L.Shuker and Miss J.J.Whiley

2013 Miss J.Griffioen and Miss A.van Koot
Miss Y.Kamiji and Miss J.J.Whiley

2014 Miss Y.Kamiji and Miss J.J.Whiley
Miss J.Griffioen and Miss A.van Koot

2015 Miss Y.Kamiji and Miss J.J.Whiley
Miss J.Griffioen and Miss A.van Koot

2016 Miss Y.Kamiji and Miss J.J.Whiley
Miss J.Griffioen and Miss A.van Koot

2017 Miss Y.Kamiji and Miss J.J.Whiley
Miss M.Buis and Miss D.de Groot

Published in 2017 by Vision Sports Publishing Ltd

Vision Sports Publishing Ltd
19-23 High Street, Kingston upon Thames
Surrey, KT1 1LL
www.visionsp.co.uk

ISBN: 978-1909534-73-5

Written by: Paul Newman
Additional writing by: Ian Chadband
Edited by: Jim Drewett and Alexandra Willis
Production editor: Ed Davis
Proofreaders: Lee Goodall, Eloise Tyson and Grace Everitt
Designed by: Neal Cobourne
Photography: Bob Martin, Thomas Lovelock, Ben Queenborough, Ben Solomon, Chris Raphael, Dave Shopland, David Levenson, Dillon Bryden, Eddie Keogh, Florian Eisele, Jed Leicester, Joe Toth, Joel Marklund, Karwai Tang, Paul Gregory, Roger Allen, Steve Lewis, Tim Clayton
Picture editors: Paul Weaver, Neil Turner, Adam Warner, Samuel Bay, Sammie Thompson, Julia Vynokurova
Picture research: Sarah Frandsen

All photographs © AELTC

Results and tables are reproduced courtesy of the AELTC

The All England Lawn Tennis Club (Championships) Limited
Church Road, Wimbledon, London, SW19 5AE, England
Tel: +44 (0)20 8944 1066
Fax: +44 (0)20 8947 8752
www.wimbledon.com

Printed in Slovakia by Neografia

This book is reproduced with the assistance of Rolex.

ROLEX